Past Masters

General Editor Keith Thomas

Hobbes

Richard Tuck is a Lecturer in History at Cambridge University and a Fellow of Jesus College. He is the author of *Natural Rights Theories* (1979).

Past Masters

Forthcoming

Richard Tuck

Hobbes

Oxford   New York

OXFORD UNIVERSITY PRESS

Oxford University Press, Walton Street, Oxford OX2 6DP

Oxford New York Toronto
Delhi Bombay Calcutta Madras Karachi
Petaling Jaya Singapore Hong Kong Tokyo
Nairobi Dar es Salaam Cape Town
Melbourne Auckland

and associated companies in
Berlin Ibadan

Oxford is a trade mark of Oxford University Press

© *Richard Tuck 1989*

First published 1989 as an Oxford University Press paperback
Reprinted 1990

British Library Cataloguing in Publication Data
Tuck, Richard, 1949–
Hobbes.
1. English philosophy. Hobbes, Thomas, 1588–1679
I. Title
192
ISBN 0–19–287668–6

Library of Congress Cataloging in Publication Data
Tuck, Richard, 1949–
Hobbes. (Past masters)
Bibliography: p.   Includes index.
1. Hobbes, Thomas, 1588–1679.   I. Title.   II. Series.
B1247.T8 1989   192   88-291148
ISBN 0–19–287668–6

Typeset by CentraCet

Printed and bound in Great Britain by
Biddles Ltd, Guildford and King's Lynn

Though words be the signs we have of one another's opinions and intentions; yet, because the equivocation of them is so frequent according to the diversity of contexture, and of the company wherewith they go (which the presence of him that speaketh, our sight of his actions, and conjecture of his intentions, must help to discharge us of): it must be extreme hard to find out the opinions and meanings of those men that are gone from us long ago, and have left no other signification thereof but their books; which cannot possibly be understood without history enough to discover those aforementioned circumstances, and also without great prudence to observe them. (Hobbes, *The Elements of Law, Natural and Politic* I.13.8)

Preface

Hobbes created English-language philosophy. Before his work, there was little written in English on the more technical areas of philosophy—on metaphysics, physics, and even ethics. Only Richard Hooker can count as a precursor, and then merely in one limited branch of philosophy, that of jurisprudence. But after Hobbes, there was no area of human enquiry deemed inappropriate for the English language. This was a remarkable achievement, and one which we tend to take for granted; but it was possible for Hobbes only because he had a thorough mastery of the contemporary debates in the traditional language of philosophy—Latin—and in the new language—French. He wrote continually in both Latin and English, and we cannot really understand his finest achievement (which was to produce, in *Leviathan*, the first unquestionably great philosophical work in our language) without surveying the full range of his intellectual activity.

This has seldom been done: of all the great philosophers, Hobbes has arguably been the most neglected by posterity. As we shall see in Part III, there are clear historical reasons for this; but the fact remains that he has suffered in many ways. He devoted at least half his time and energy to trying to understand modern science, at the moment at which it was first emerging; his understanding of it was certainly as acute as any of his contemporaries; yet because his ideas on this subject are not fully discussed in *Leviathan* his theories are disregarded. The works in which he set them out are scarcely read today, and some of them have not even been translated from their original Latin. Though *Leviathan* is remarkable in many ways, it was not actually intended by him to be his principal statement even on political and moral matters, and our (understandable) concentration on that single work has distorted many accounts of what Hobbes was trying to do.

Hobbes is thus a peculiarly appropriate figure to be discussed in a book of this kind, for the resurrection of what he was

trying to do yields intellectual dividends well beyond the area
of pure historical enquiry. But he is also an unusually difficult
figure, for most present-day readers of Hobbes approach him
with expectations formed either wittingly or unwittingly by
the unsatisfactory traditions of interpretation which have
developed about him during the last two centuries. I have
therefore divided the body of the book into three parts. In the
first, I have described his life (an astonishing and often tumul-
tuous one) and the broad intellectual contexts in which he
operated at different phases of his life. This part offers in effect
a brief, synoptic view of Hobbes's philosophy. The second part
then focuses more closely on the arguments advanced in his
philosophical works, considering them as contributions to
contemporary debates on science, ethics, politics, and religion.
The last part considers in more detail the post-Hobbesian
interpretations of these arguments, and compares them with
the account of the arguments I have offered in Part II. Hobbes's
modern commentators have, I believe, made him both more
difficult and less interesting than he deserves, and locating him
more firmly in the debates of his own time emphasizes rather
than diminishes his importance in the debates of our century.

Many people have helped in the construction of this book,
notably the undergraduates with whom I have discussed
Hobbes over the past fifteen years (especially my present
Special Subject group of historians in Cambridge), and my
former colleague Noel Malcolm, whose knowledge of Hobbes
is unparalleled. But I owe the following a particular debt for
reading the manuscript of the book and commenting on it:
Quentin Skinner, James Tully, Anne Malcolm, J. P. Tuck, and
the general editor of the Past Masters series, Keith Thomas. All
of them made me think again about important aspects of the
work, and prevented many errors and infelicities from reaching
a wider audience.

Contents

I Hobbes's life

The life of a humanist

It is sometimes tempting to think that the heroes of the various histories of philosophy or ethics—men as different as St Thomas Aquinas, Machiavelli, Luther, Hobbes, Kant, or Hegel—were all in some sense engaged on a common enterprise, and would have recognized one another as fellow workers. But a moment's reflection reminds us that it is we who have made a unity of their task: from their own point of view, they belonged to very different ways of living and had very different tasks to perform. They would have seen themselves as intellectually kin to men who do not figure in these lists—priests or scholars who had on the face of it no great philosophical interest. This is particularly true of the major philosophers of late sixteenth- and seventeenth-century Europe; many of them were trained as what were termed 'humanists', and their intellectual origins lay in the study of the classics and in the stylish and imaginative use of language characteristic of the early Renaissance humanists, rather than in the laborious philosophizing of their medieval precursors. The life of an intellectual in seventeenth-century Europe, in both its material conditions and its theoretical concerns, would have been immediately recognizable to a humanist of the early sixteenth century, but would have seemed very strange to a scholastic philosopher of the late Middle Ages.

Of no one is this truer than Hobbes. He was born into a relatively poor family, like many seventeenth-century writers—only Descartes and Robert Boyle, of all the throng of philosophers and scientists which the century produced, came from unimpeachably upper-class backgrounds. His father was an impoverished minor clergyman in the town of Malmesbury (Wiltshire), the kind of ecclesiastic left over from pre-Elizabethan times who was not even (almost certainly) a graduate. He was also an alcoholic who deserted his family when Thomas

1

was sixteen, to die (as Aubrey, Hobbes's wonderful biographer, and friend, recorded rather oddly) 'in obscurity beyond London'. Hobbes was born on 5 April 1588, and he seems to have been fond of repeating the joke that his mother fell into labour with him on hearing a rumour that the Spanish Armada was coming—'so that fear and I were born twins together'.

He was clearly recognized very early as an extremely clever boy, particularly at mastering the Renaissance curriculum of a sixteenth-century grammar school with its emphasis on a fluent and stylish grasp of Latin and, though to a lesser extent, Greek. Hobbes was a very fine linguist who could both speak and read Latin, Greek, French, and Italian as well as English. While still at school he translated Euripides' *Medea* from Greek into Latin iambics, and an interest in and a proficiency at translation accompanied him for the rest of his life. His first publication was in fact a translation into English of Thucydides (1629), and one of his last was a translation of the *Odyssey* into English verse. This also reflects the other skill which a Renaissance grammar school sought to impart to its pupils, and in which Hobbes was again spectacularly fluent—the writing of poetry. His first known written work to survive is a Latin poem on 'the Wonders of the English Peak in Darby-shire', and all his life he wrote Latin and English verse. He was, it should be said, in general an extremely quick writer of both prose and verse, once he put his mind to any project (though he also accused himself of laziness)—we know, for example, that he wrote the last ten chapters of *Leviathan* (about 90,000 words) in considerably less than a year.

These skills were not, in sixteenth- and seventeenth-century Europe, what they subsequently became—the resolutely impractical badge of a social élite. They had become embedded in the school curriculum since the Renaissance because they had a use, and were in fact highly marketable; proficiency at them offered a fine means of social advancement for a bright, lower-class boy. Clearly, the ancient professions—the Church, the Law and Medicine—recruited people of this sort; but there was a much wider demand for them, since anyone who was engaged in public life (particularly if that public life involved a knowledge of or participation in the wider European context) needed men about him who were good linguists and fluent and persuasive writers, capable of conducting correspondence, drafting speeches, giving advice, and training up children in the same skills. This was the market for 'humanism' as the word had been understood since the Renaissance, and it was the prevalence of such people in the city states and princely courts of Italy which had first fostered the development of Renaissance culture. But the same kind of men existed in Northern Europe, particularly in the great aristocratic families, and surprisingly many major seventeenth-century writers lived as the pensioners of such families (John Locke and John Selden are two notable examples).

It was into the household of one of these aristocrats that Hobbes was recruited, after passing from the Malmesbury school to an Oxford 'hall' (a kind of college entirely devoted to the general Arts course, rather than the specialized postgraduate professional courses). It may well be that, like Locke later, Hobbes felt a strong and principled reluctance to enter a profession, and particularly the largest employer of graduates, the Church; his hostility to all the professions was later most marked, and was something which earlier humanists too had often exhibited (it is no accident that most of the famous early Italian humanists were laymen). The household of a great English nobleman offered a different kind of life, though one with some social costs: it made a married life virtually impossible, and it is striking how many of the great seventeenth-century theorists were bachelors, living a life without close ties of affection; Locke is again an obvious case. Such households would disengage a theorist not merely from family ties, but from many of the institutions in which most people lived their lives, and would naturally breed a radical and self-confident race of intellectuals. And while they also continually emphasized the difference in social status between nobleman and employee—Hobbes referred to himself on occasion as a 'domestic' in the household of his employer—they did so while simultaneously putting the servant and the master on an intellectual level, leading to (in our eyes) a strangely ambiguous relationship.

The nobleman to whom the recently graduated Hobbes was recommended in February 1608 by the Principal of his hall was William Lord Cavendish, created Earl of Devonshire in 1618, who despite his title lived principally at Hardwick Hall in Derbyshire. The rest of Hobbes's life was spent in the employment either of the Earls of Devonshire, or their neighbours and cousins the Earls of Newcastle (or, briefly, another of their neighbouring families). He acted as secretary, tutor, financial agent, and general adviser, and we have one or two vivid glimpses of his life during the next twenty years. Like all such servants, he spent a lot of time sitting in anterooms while his master and other great men discussed state affairs (or merely gossiped), and Aubrey recorded that to while away the time he would read the pocket-sized editions of classical texts produced by the Dutch printers Elzevir. In the anterooms he would meet the secretaries of other noblemen, and some of Hobbes's disappointingly scanty correspondence from this period is with such secretaries and tutors, full of private jokes about their masters' doings. Because his master disliked financial affairs, Hobbes sat as his nominee on the board of the Virginia Company in which the Devonshires had a substantial holding. And when Lord Cavendish sent his son off on what would later be called 'the Grand Tour' between 1610 and 1615, Hobbes accompanied him as a tutor, though only three years separated pupil and tutor—another finely-judged and ambiguous relationship.

Touring round Europe as what one of his French friends later called the 'conducteur d'un Seigneur' became in fact one of Hobbes's major activities: in addition to the 1610–15 trip, he took the son of another family round Europe in 1630, and in 1634–6 he took the son of his pupil of 1610 on a journey similar to the one he had gone on with his father. These tours gave Hobbes an opportunity to meet both politicians and intellectuals throughout Europe which probably no other major thinker has ever enjoyed; by 1636 he had met most of the leading philosophers of his time, from Galileo (whom he probably met at Florence in the spring of 1636) to the French-men Pierre Gassendi and Marin Mersenne—the latter was the only effective channel of communication with René Descartes (who was virtually in hiding in The Netherlands at the time), and he put Hobbes and Descartes in touch, though they did not actually meet until 1648.

But Hobbes was not particularly interested in such figures until the 1630s; what seems to have had the greatest impact on him in his early trips was his visit to Venice, where his master became acquainted with some of the principal writer-politi-cians of the Republic, who had recently defended its indepen-dence from the Papacy and the Hapsburgs in the 'Interdict Crisis' of 1606. When Hobbes and Cavendish returned to England, they kept in touch with these Venetians (Hobbes, characteristically, translating their letters from Italian to Eng-lish so that his master could read them), and for some time the Venetians' concerns became those of the Cavendish household also. Many of the themes which emerged at this time were to play an important part, though often metamorphosed, in Hobbes's later works.

Venice was the only survivor from the great days of Italian republicanism, and the men who controlled it were obsessed, reasonably enough, with the question of what had led other Italian republics such as Florence to collapse into principalities effectively under the domination of Spain—which since its victory in the Italian wars of the early sixteenth century had imposed a system of formal and informal imperial control across the Peninsula, pulling the city-states into line with a combination of financial bribery, military intimidation, and propaganda about the threat from the Turkish Empire. Seen from Venice, and indeed from many other vantage points in Europe, this process (together with the comparable attempt by the Spaniards to maintain control of The Netherlands) was the quintessence of modern politics, and a whole *genre* of works on politics developed to analyse it. This was the kind of political literature with which the young Hobbes was most familiar; it was a particularly appealing *genre* for a humanist since it continually deployed classical themes and quoted ancient authors—and indeed some of the contributors to it were among the leading classical scholars of their time.

The central feature of this literature was a pervasive scepticism about the validity of the moral principles by which an earlier generation had lived. For writers of that earlier generation, in the late fifteenth or early sixteenth centuries, an effective public life lived by honourable men was still a possibility; and whether they were citizens of a republic such as Florence before the Medici, or advisers to a prince such as the Duke of Milan, the King of France or the Emperor Charles V, they found models for what they sought in the works of ancient writers who had followed the same vision—notably Cicero and Seneca. The idea that something like the Ciceronian republic could be reconstructed in modern Europe took an extraordinary hold on the imagination of many men at the beginning of the sixteenth century, and led some people (like the Italian Cardinal Bembo) to purge even their language of all post-Ciceronian accretions (which made writing a history of Venice, as Bembo did, rather difficult—for example, the Turks had become 'Thracians', and the nunneries of the city 'temples of vestal virgins').

But this Ciceronian ideal, vividly though it is expressed in the art and literature of Renaissance Italy, came by the end of the century to seem nothing more than a fantasy. The reality of modern politics was manipulation, deceit, and intimidation, and the classical author who captured this was not Cicero but Tacitus. One of the major theorists of this new attitude was the Netherlander Justus Lipsius, who said of Tacitus in 1574:

> this writer deals with princely courts, with the inner life of princes, . . . and he teaches us, who have noticed the similarity in many respects with our own times, that the same effects may come from the same causes. You will find under a tyrant flattery and treachery not unknown in our age; nothing sincere, nothing straightforward, and not even good faith amongst friends; constant accusations of treason . . .; mass slaughter of good men, and a peace more brutal than war.

Machiavelli, though himself in many ways an authentic Ciceronian, was reread by a new audience in the last decades of the sixteenth century as a kind of Tacitist, and his fellow-countryman Guicciardini was admired even more—largely because, far more than Machiavelli, he expressed a sceptical disengagement from politics. A term that Guicciardini first used became in time a watchword for this new movement: it was *ragion di stato*, 'reason of state', which appears in the titles of books and pamphlets all over Europe from about 1590 onwards.

However, the sense that honour and morality had departed from the world had wider implications than the merely political. Not only had the practical circumstances of modernity rendered traditional ethics irrelevant, they had called into question the validity of ethical commitments *as such*. Right across Europe, for example, the Wars of Religion after the Reformation had been fought to a standstill, with neither side achieving an outright victory: almost all European countries were now going to have to live with a substantial degree of fundamental ideological conflict within their boundaries. It would be hard to overestimate the shock which the warfare between religious fanatics caused to disengaged contemporary observers; as Lipsius said,

> Good Lord, what firebrands of sedition hath religion kindled in this fayrest part of the world? The chiefe heads of our christian commonwealths are at strife amongst them selves, and many millions of men have bin brought to ruine and do dayly perish, under a pretext of piety.

The response of many of Lipsius's generation (he was born in 1547) was to give up strongly held and publicly defended beliefs of all kinds, and to retreat to a dispassionate and sceptical stance. Here, too, they found ancient exemplars: the collapse of the free Greek city-states of antiquity in the face of the empires first of Alexander and his successors, and then of Rome, had engendered a very similar set of attitudes. The sceptics in the ancient world such as Pyrrho or Carneades argued that nothing could be known securely about either the moral or the physical world: knowledge of the former was vitiated by irresolvable disagreement between different cultures and ages, while knowledge of the latter was prevented by the varying and inaccurate character of human observation (optical illusions, etc.). They urged instead the cultivation of what they called *ataraxia*, the complete suspension of belief and consequently of all emotional involvement with anything. To an extent, scepticism of this kind joined hands with another ancient philosophy, Stoicism: for while the Stoics did not rule out the possibility of knowledge, they also stressed that the path of wisdom was the elimination of emotion and passionate commitment, and the entering into a state of *apatheia*.

In the late sixteenth century, both sceptical and Stoic texts were widely read; Lipsius made himself an expert not merely on Tacitus but on Stoicism also, and he often expressed a sympathy with the ancient sceptics. His closest intellectual ally, the Frenchman Michel de Montaigne (about whom Lipsius once said, 'I have found no one in Europe whose way of thinking about things is closer to my own'), achieved great fame in his *Essais* of 1580–8 precisely by blending Tacitism, scepticism, and Stoicism in an enticing and persuasive mixture; he provided what might stand as a summary of the fundamental attitude when he said in a rightly famous passsage,

> what goodnesse is that, which but yesterday I saw in credit and esteeme, and to morrow, to have lost all reputation, and that the crossing of a River, is made a crime? What truth is that, which these Mountains bound, and is a lie in the World beyond them?

One universal principle of human conduct remained intact after this sceptical onslaught, however. It was that men both do and must seek their own *self-preservation*. Both Montaigne and Lipsius condemned public-spiritedness and patriotism, for such feelings exposed their possessor to great danger: the wise man took his own survival to be his central obligation, and would do nothing and cultivate no feelings which might endanger it. Moreover, if he had in the end to choose between his own survival and that of another, he must choose his own.

Here, again, they were echoing antiquity: the second-century B.C. sceptic Carneades had argued forcefully that in the event of a shipwreck, the wise man would be prepared to seize the only plank capable of bearing him to shore, even if that meant pushing another person off it.

A further parallel between the ancient world and the modern lay in the character of the target against which these arguments were levelled. In the ancient world, the most complete and systematic body of knowledge or 'science' was represented by the works of Arsitotle, and it was against Aristotle and his followers that both sceptic and Stoic repeatedly turned. Aristotle had, for example, asserted that, all other things being equal, human perceptions of the external world were *correct*: if something *looks* white to an ordinary, healthy observer, then it *is* white. The sceptical stress on optical illusion and the generally unreliable character of sense-perception obviously undermined the whole of Aristotelian science. Likewise, Aristotle had expressed great confidence in the universality of (roughly) the conventional moral beliefs of a middle-class Athenian of his day, and it was easy to cast doubt on this by pointing to the astonishing diversity of ethical belief and conduct in the world.

For the writers of the late sixteenth century, too, Aristotle was one of the principal targets; both Protestant and Catholic had sought to align their certainties with his, and the whole Aristotelian enterprise gave people confidence that a determinate and valid body of knowledge was possible. Though the Ciceronians of Renaissance Italy had condemned the medieval Aristotelians, they had not in general condemned the historical Aristotle, and a new school of post-Renaissance Aristotelian studies sprang up in the early sixteenth century. But Lipsius, Montaigne, and their followers were intemperate in their attacks on Aristotle himself; as one of these followers, the Frenchman Pierre Charron, said in 1601, Aristotle 'hath uttered more grosse absurdities than [any other philosopher], and is at no agreement with himself, neither doth he know many times where he is'.

These, then, were the attitudes to modern politics which

seemed to many people early in the seventeenth century best to capture the realities of their situation. In Venice, all these themes were discussed: Paolo Sarpi, leader of the Republic during the Interdict Crisis, was a keen reader of Montaigne and a clear sceptic in his own right, while another propagandist for Venice (Trajano Boccalini) praised both Lipsius and Tacitus extensively. What in particular they found admirable in these modern authors was their disengagement from *religious* belief: Venice was struggling to maintain its independence in religious matters from the Papacy, and the Venetian state sought to keep a firm grip on religious enthusiasm in the city. Sarpi, despite being a Servite friar, went so far as to argue that a community of atheists could funtion perfectly well as a civil society, and he and his fellows were impressed when they read Francis Bacon's *Essays* (modelled on Montaigne, and influenced by Lipsius) to discover that he thought the same: 'atheism leaves a man to sense, to philosophy, to natural piety, to laws, to reputation; all which may be guides to an outward moral virtue, though religion were not; . . . we see the times inclined to atheism (as the time of Augustus Caesar) were civil times' (Essay XVII, 'Of Superstition').

Accordingly, they urged the translation of Bacon's *Essays* into Latin so that a wider European audience could read them, and were keen to keep in touch with Cavendish and Hobbes in order to use them as a channel of communication with Bacon. A letter of 1623 asked Cavendish to find someone who could act as an amanuensis for Bacon and then send information about his new ideas out to Venice. It is no surprise, therefore, to find Aubrey recording that Hobbes both translated several of Bacon's *Essays* into Latin, and took down his thoughts as Bacon dictated them while walking in his garden at Gorhambury. The Cavendish household also went in for writing Bacon-like essays on various subjects, a volume of which survives; it was once thought to be by Hobbes, but it is now thought that it was in fact by his pupil.

The Venetians were also keen on the study of the Greek historian Thucydides. While admiring Tacitus, they recognized that he dealt with the affairs of a monarchy, not a republic; in

Thucydides' history of the war between Athens and Sparta they found the appropriate text for a modern republic—far from the noble tone of Cicero, and suitably sceptical and relativist about human affairs. One of Sarpi's friends tried to persuade scholars throughout Europe to study Thucydides, and again it is no surprise to find that in 1629 Hobbes appeared in print for the first time with an English translation of Thucydides dedicated to the young third Earl of Devonshire in memory of his father (Hobbes's pupil on the Venetian trip), who had died prematurely the previous year, and that in the introduction to it he praised Lipsius.

The culture of modern humanism into which he had thus incorporated himself was to remain important to Hobbes for the rest of his life, though, as we shall see, he distanced himself from many of its specific elements, and in particular its openness to classical republicanism. Indeed, in one sense his life's work, at least in political theory, can be read as a transformation of this culture from within: what for Lipsius and Montaigne had been an ineluctable and natural principle of human conduct, namely self-preservation, becomes in Hobbes the fundamental *right* upon which a new kind of ethics can be constructed. But he embarked on this enterprise only after assimilating a rather different kind of intellectual culture, in which the study of metaphysics and physics played a far more prominent role than they had done in the humanist circles of his youth.

The life of a philosopher

The second Earl of Devonshire having died shortly before the translation of Thucydides was published, Hobbes found himself effectively without employment: the third Earl was only eleven on his father's death, and Hobbes did not belong in a fatherless household of young children. For a couple of years he acted as tutor in a neighbouring house, and then returned to the Devonshires to act as adviser to the Dowager Countess and tutor to the Earl. At the same time he came to be more closely associated with another branch of the Cavendish family, settled at Welbeck, about eight miles from Hardwick, and headed by the Earl of Newcastle. He now began to act as agent and adviser for these Cavendishes also, and their interests pushed him in a new direction, away from his purely humanistic skills.

Both the Earl of Newcastle and his younger brother Sir Charles Cavendish were primarily concerned with military affairs: the Earl, indeed, became one of the principal Royalist generals on the outbreak of the Civil War in 1642. In early seventeenth-century Europe, there was virtually an entire way of life centred on the army: the war against Spain in The Netherlands, which had led to the independence of the Dutch republic in the late sixteenth century, gradually spread out across the Continent and became enmeshed with other wars and revolutions against Hapsburg power such as the Bohemian Revolt of 1618, until almost the whole of Europe was caught up in what was later termed the Thirty Years War (1618–48). England is usually thought to have been only marginally involved in this conflict, but in fact there was a substantial English army in Holland almost continuously from 1584 to 1642.

The miliary culture of early seventeenth-century Europe owed a lot to the modern humanism surveyed in the previous section. Lipsius, once again, was a leading theorist of both the Roman and the modern army, his works on military organisation and discipline being eagerly read even by field commanders. A contemporary critic of Tacitism even observed that Tacitus's prose style sounded like the clipped commands of a soldier, quite different from the orotund and peaceful prose of Cicero. But the military culture went beyond humanism in its interest in science and technology (though Lipsius did write a book on Roman military machines). The great new armies of the period fought with up-to-date weapons, particularly battlefield artillery, and a proper understanding of how the new technology worked was vital to effective soldiering.

The Earl of Newcastle and his brother had a consuming interest in military technology. The Earl was particularly concerned with horses (which were of course still centrally important in warfare), but he was also interested in the modern study of *optics*, especially its application to the development of an effective telescope—a tremendously important military prize for the first nation to develop one. It should be remembered that the very first, primitive telescope was constructed as late as 1608, by the Dutchman Lippershey. Sir Charles was himself a competent mathematician, and interested in both optics and ballistics (the development of modern mathematical dynamics and military fire-power going hand in hand). But the two brothers were also clearly interested in some of the fundamental theoretical issues thrown up by the new technologies, and corresponded with or helped financially philosophers and scientists both in England and on the Continent.

As an intermittent servant of the Earl of Newcastle, Hobbes found himself during the 1630s pursuing his master's interests in these areas. Thus he was sent off to look at horses and buy them on Newcastle's behalf; one of the odder productions of his pen was a theoretical analysis of the gaits of a horse which he produced for the Earl, but never published. In January 1634, while visiting London with 'My Lady' (that is, the Dowager Countess of Devonshire), Hobbes was commissioned by Newcastle to buy a copy of Galileo's *Dialogue Concerning the Two Chief Systems of the World* (1632), the foundational work of modern physics—the first indication that Hobbes was becoming involved in these concerns. During 1634 he discussed problems of optics and physics with people associated with the Welbeck Cavendishes, and when he took the young third Earl of Devonshire off on his Grand Tour later that year he also took with him letters of introduction from the Cavendishes to various French mathematicians and philosophers. Because of the importance of his young charge, he even obtained an invitation to meet Galileo himself at Arcetri near Florence. This journey, which lasted until October 1636, seems to have been one of the key periods in Hobbes's life, overshadowing even the Venetian visit of 1610.

It was at this time that he became aware of what was happening in French philosophical circles. The heart of French philosophy at this time was in a chamber of the convent of the Minim Friars in Paris, occupied by Father Marin Mersenne, whom Hobbes later described as 'the pole round which revolved

13

every star in the world of science'. Mersenne both kept in touch with savants all over Europe, and seems to have had a clear vision himself of what a new philosophy must consist in. All the philosophers whose work he applauded and orchestrated differed from the humanist sceptics of the previous generation in that they believed that science of various kinds was possible. As we saw in the previous section, late sixteenth-century scepticism had called into question the possibility of ever having a true and systematic knowledge of *anything*: both the natural and the moral world were seen as essentially unknowable. But the philosophers round Mersenne rejected this pessimism, without in any way wishing to revert to traditional Aristotelianism. They had before them an example of a new kind of science, explicitly anti-Aristotelian but also transcending scepticism, in the shape of Galileo's physics; the philosophers following in his wake sought, in effect, to retain the critical insights of late Renaissance humanism (and much of its substantive content in the way of theories of language, political conduct, etc.), but to marry to them the new natural science of Galileo. Although, as we shall see, they came to hope that a new *ethical* science could be developed too, this seems to have been initially less important for them.

Mersenne himself published in 1625 a book on *Scientific Truth: Against the Sceptics or Pyrrhonians*, in which he sought to answer the sceptical case against the possibility of a wide range of sciences without returning to Aristotelianism; but his arguments were *ad hoc* and clearly unsatisfactory. However, one of his friends was able to accomplish what Mersenne hoped for: this was the famous René Descartes, who had actually been at school with Mersenne. Descartes was from a noble family, and had followed the calling of a soldier; indeed, he later alleged that his fundamental philosophical idea came to him while in winter quarters on one of the campaigns of the Thirty Years War. During the 1630s he was effectively in hiding in Holland, working on his philosophy and communicating with the outside world only through Mersenne. Between 1629 and 1633 he composed his first major work, *The World*, in which some of his ideas were put forward; but in it he committed himself to supporting Galileo's theory that the earth rotated, and news of Galileo's condemnation at the hands of the Roman Inquisition in 1633 led him to abandon publication of the book. However, much of the material that would have been in it appeared four years later in a collection of essays prefaced by *A Discourse on the Method for Rightly Conducting the Reason and Searching for Truth in the Sciences*, one of the most famous pieces of philosophical writing.

To understand Descartes's arguments (and, later, the comparable arguments of Hobbes), we must remember that the sceptical attack on natural science had emphasized the impossibility of accurate observation of the external world: since we are familiar with optical illusions, dreams, and so on, how do we know that what we see *really* has the properties which we ascribe to it? And if we cannot know that, how can we know the truth about anything? The answers these seventeenth-century philosophers gave to these questions might seem very simple to us, but that is because they have become the foundational presuppositions of our scientific culture. Descartes and his contemporaries were living in a culture saturated by Aristotelianism, where, if one was not a total sceptic, one was likely to believe that the external world actually possessed the properties ascribed to it by an observer, so that anything which, for example, looked red was really red, in the same sense that it might be said to be really a certain size or shape.

Descartes, however, denied this, without becoming a complete sceptic. Instead, he insisted that there need be no resemblance between what we experience and the external world: the sequence of images that constitutes our continuous life of perception does not necessarily represent in a picture-like way the world outside us. In *The World* he used the analogy of language: words refer to objects, but they do not *resemble* them; in the same way, he argued, visual images or other sensory inputs relate to objects without depicting them. The external world is in fact incapable of being experienced in its true character. By contrast, we can have an absolutely compelling knowledge of our own internal life, and of the images which flicker in front of us.

The difference between Descartes and a sceptic arose from this last point, and it is a subtle but nevertheless crucial divergence. For the sceptics, the fact that one person thought an apple was green and another thought it was brown illustrated our incapacity to know the truth: the apple, they believed, must be a determinate colour, but human perception could not decide what it was. To that extent, the sceptic was still a kind of Aristotelian, who simply insisted on the irremediable character of human fallibility: an ideal, non-human observer might see the world as it really was, and it would still be a world of colours, smells, tastes, and so on. Descartes, on the other hand, argued that we have no reason to suppose that there are colours, etc., in the real, external world *at all*, and therefore no reason to conclude that colour-blindness (for example) means that we cannot know the truth about that world. Colour is solely an internal phenomenon, caused no doubt by something external, but neither fallibly nor infallibly representing it.

Descartes was not actually the first person to come up with this idea. Something quite like it appears in a book which another friend of Mersenne's, Pierre Gassendi, wrote in 1625, but did not publish until 1649, while Hobbes also persistently claimed that he had had the same idea independently of both Descartes and Gassendi, in 1630. But though none of these three ever acknowledged as much, the idea in fact first appeared in print (applied to the sensation of heat rather than colour, but the principle is the same) in a work by Galileo of 1623, *The Assayer*. Descartes himself alleged in *A Discourse on the Method* that he had first had the idea in 1619, partly perhaps to register a prior claim to Galileo. Unfortunately, there is no corroboration for the claims of either Hobbes or Descartes. What is clear, however, is that like scientists today competing for a Nobel Prize, these philosophers were conscious of the great importance of the discovery and anxious to claim unique credit for it.

In one sense this idea answered the sceptic, but in another it engendered a new kind of scepticism, throwing doubt even on the *existence* of properties like colour. There is no question but that it was Descartes who was chiefly responsible for seeing this and exploring its implications. Between writing *The World* and *A Discourse on the Method* he was led to consider further the sceptical aspect of his idea, and in the latter work he was to present a notorious new doubt. Perhaps not only colours are non-existent, but also the material objects in which they seem to inhere? Perhaps there is *nothing* out there: after all, we can imagine a language which is complete in itself but which does not refer to any real objects (like the languages which Tolkien invented to accompany *The Lord of the Rings*), so why can we not imagine an orderly and systematic sequence of images which do not refer to anything? Dreams, Descartes pointed out, are precisely such sequences. The consequences of abandoning both Aristotelianism and traditional scepticism thus appeared vertiginous, leading to a form of scepticism more alarming than any before, in which the entire external world melted away.

At the beginning of *A Discourse* Descartes presented this doubt, along with more traditional doubts culled from the sceptical literature; he then sought to answer it, claiming that if this 'hyperbolical' doubt could be answered, the traditional ones would also collapse—though he had actually little reason to suppose this was the case. His answer rested on two arguments. The first was expressed in the slogan *Cogito ergo sum* ('I think therefore I am'): though there may be nothing outside, we know there is something inside, for we have direct experience of the interior world of colours, sounds, and so on. The puzzle is, does this interior world relate to anything external? Here Descartes used his second argument, which was an a priori 'proof' of God's existence (that is, a 'proof' which purports to need no information about the external world for its validity). Having to his own satisfaction established the existence of a God of a familiar kind—that is, a benevolent creator—Descartes concluded that such a God would not mislead his favoured creation, man. What we genuinely think we perceive must therefore be more or less what is actually out there.

The elegance with which Descartes presented his doubt

excited readers all over Europe; but the cogency of his answer was less apparent. As both Gassendi and Hobbes later pointed out, the argument for God's existence was very shaky, and if that was removed Descartes turned out to be a super-sceptic. Instead of doing the work Mersenne and the others hoped for, of vindicating the natural sciences, *A Discourse on the Method* then looked more like a demonstration of their wholly imaginary character. Science would (in our terms) be indistinguishable from science fiction. So a major task still remained for modern philosophy, and Hobbes, with characteristic intellectual self-confidence, appears to have decided after reading *A Discourse on the Method* that he would shoulder the burden.

What he produced at this point remained in manuscript, in some cases down to the twentieth century, and much has also been lost, so the true story of his first attempts at philosophy will probably never be known. The story in modern works on Hobbes is unnecessarily complicated by the fact that one of the great Hobbes scholars, the German Ferdinand Toennies, attributed to Hobbes in 1889 a manuscript in the British Museum known as 'A Short Tract on First Principles', and dated it to *c*.1630—the time when Hobbes claimed to have first thought of his theory of perception. Unfortunately, though all subsequent writers have followed Toennies, there is in fact no evidence that the manuscript is by Hobbes, let alone that it dates from *c*.1630; it also contains some arguments which directly contradict what Hobbes said was his fundamental idea. For these reasons I shall not refer to it again.

The secure evidence points to the following account. In the mid-1630s Hobbes followed the lead of the Earl of Newcastle and Sir Charles Cavendish into the modern study of optics and ballistics, becoming in the process as dissatisfied with conventional Aristotelian physics as he had earlier been with Aristotelian ethics. Even before reading Descartes, he had come to fundamentally the same conclusion as Descartes and Gassendi about perception; in a letter to the Earl in October 1636 about light passing through a pinhole, he remarked that 'whereas I use the phrases, the light passes, or the coulor [sic] passes or diffuseth itselfe, my meaning is that the motion is onely in the medium, and light and coulor are but the effects of that motion in the brayne'. A year later a friend in Paris sent Hobbes a copy of Descartes's *Discourse*, in which Hobbes read of the sceptical use to which this idea could be put.

During the next three years Hobbes worked away on his philosophy, and by the end of 1640 (when, as we shall see, he had to flee to France) he had written two drafts. One was a fairly substantial work in Latin, divided into three 'Sections'. Section One was devoted to the fundamentals of metaphysics and physics—to such questions as the nature of space, matter, motion, and so on. Section Two was concerned with perception, and included a long discussion of the principles of optics (reflection, refraction, etc.), as well as other aspects of human conduct such as the desire for what is perceived and the judgement that it is 'good'. Section Three dealt with the political implications of these arguments. Hobbes seems to have intended that the overall title of the work should be *The Elements of Philosophy*. All that clearly survives of this early draft is part of Section Two (a manuscript formerly in Sir Charles Cavendish's possession and now in the British Museum), but we can tell from that fragment that a critique of Descartes was fundamental to it: Descartes's optics are criticized on almost every page.

The second of these two early drafts survives entire, indeed in many manuscript copies. It was a work in English which essentially put into a single compass what Hobbes had put in Sections Two and Three of the Latin *Elements of Philosophy*; he gave it the title *The Elements of Law, Natural and Politic*. It is characteristic of Hobbes that he should have workd on the same material simultaneously in English and Latin: this bilingual approach remained a feature of his work, and reflects his fluency and interest in translation. The *Elements of Law* was apparently written quite quickly, with the political events of 1640 very much in his mind, and it was widely circulated among his English friends; in the eyes of many of them, and of many subsequent readers, it remains one of the best statements of Hobbes's philosophy.

From the point of view of his French friends, for whom the

Latin *Elements of Philosophy* was presumably intended, the most striking thing about both drafts would have been the last sections, on politics. Though Descartes had rather vaguely proclaimed his intention of putting both ethics and politics on a new foundation, he conspicuously failed to do so, and remained one of the few major philosophers never to write on politics. Nor is there much indication, in Hobbes's correspondence with Newcastle and Newcastle's scientists in the mid-1630s, that he was then vitally concerned with political matters. But his move to include politics in his survey of philosophy is not in fact surprising, particularly given the form he gave to it—that is, an account of the elements of *law*, with the principles of *natural law* at its heart.

It is not surprising because there already existed a major work of legal philosophy which was extremely well suited in a number of respects to Hobbes's general purpose of transcending scepticism. It could play the same role for him as Galileo's *Dialogues* did for all the members of the Mersenne circle, as a representation for them of the kind of science which was to be put on their new, post-sceptical foundations. This work was Hugo Grotius's *The Laws of War and Peace*, published in 1625. Grotius was a Dutchman; only five years older than Hobbes, he already had an immense reputation across Europe. Like Hobbes, he had been a skilled humanist in his youth, and had been recruited to serve as an aide to one of the statesmen of his nation. But a remarkable career in Dutch politics culminated in 1619 with his being tried for treason, and nearly condemned to death; he escaped from prison, and spent the rest of his life in exile. As a young man he had been open to the humanism of Lipsius and Montaigne, but he gradually came to see that something new was required; in a series of works drafted in the first and second decades of the century he developed a new ethical theory, and from 1625 that theory was fully in the public domain.

Though *The Laws of War and Peace* is a long and discursive work, its fundamental argument is quite simple. It begins by posing the sceptical challenge to conventional ethics, through a summary of the views of the ancient sceptic Carneades, and then tries to answer the challenge—just as Descartes began by raising his doubt and then replied to it. Grotius's answer was in effect that whatever else they believed or had believed in the past, all men would agree that everyone has a fundamental *right* to preserve themselves, and that wanton or unnecessary injury to another person is unjustifiable. No social life was possible if the members of a society denied either of these two propositions, but no other principles were necessary for a social existence, at least on a rudimentary level.

Grotius made it clear that this theory was directed both at the sceptic and at the Aristotelian. It answered the sceptic because it showed that the multiplicity of beliefs and practices around the world was compatible with a minimal common core of morality, and it rebutted the Aristotelian because it disregarded the elaborate accounts of the virtues and the principles of natural law which Aristotelians had always sought to develop. Such things as *benevolence*, for example—actually helping one's neighbour, as distinct from not injuring him—were put by Grotius on a higher level than the minimal core: one could envisage a society of rather stand-offish individuals who had no sense of common welfare beyond the common security of their own persons. International relations, according to Grotius, provided an example of just such a society: nation-states were under no obligation to help one another, but they were obliged not to harm each other; and much of his book was devoted to exploring the implications of this observation.

Three features of Grotius's work were particularly significant for Hobbes's enterprise. The first was that Grotius had in a sense converted the sceptical humanist's language of self-preservation into a language of *natural rights*—that is, into a genuinely *moral* language—without abandoning much of the actual content of the theories put forward by men such as Lipsius and Montaigne. Theories based on natural rights were to be the principal vehicles for the discussion of ethical issues for the rest of the century. Second, Grotius (unlike Descartes) had accomplished this conversion without talking about God; in fact, in a notorious passage he said that his thesis would hold good 'even if we should concede (what cannot be conceded

21

without great wickedness) that there is no God'. Grotius had met the sceptic on his own ground: if the source of the sceptic's dismay was his perception of the multiplicity of human beliefs, that dismay could be countered simply by pointing to something all human beings must have in common.

But in some ways it was the third feature which was most significant. Grotius's minimal core of rights and duties gave rise to a 'state of nature' (though he did not himself often use this term), a state in which *all* men must find themselves simply *qua* men, and on to which would be grafted the various appurtenances of developed civil life, including benevolence. Thus whatever rights or duties were claimed by governments must have arisen from or be compatible with the rights and duties of the state of nature. In this sense Grotius was a thorough-going individualist: no political community could have any moral hold over its members unless those members had in some way given it that moral hold. This, too, was to be chracteristic of much political thought in the course of the century.

The use to which Grotius put his new theory of natural rights was also suggestive. We are accustomed, perhaps, to thinking of natural rights as a *liberal* doctrine, and to associating them with such things as the American Declaration of Independence—the 'rights of man'. But for Grotius, as for many of his early followers, the implications of the minimalist theory of natural rights were *illiberal*. *All* we have the fundamental right to do is to preserve ourselves; whatever is necessary to our preservation (without, at least according to Grotius, endangering other people's preservation) is *ipso facto* legitimate. He gave two examples of this: one was voluntary slavery, in which someone on the verge of starvation or execution sells himself to a master in return for his life and food, and the other was absolute monarchy, where an entire population might renounce their civil rights in order to achieve social peace or prosperity. It is worth remembering that the latter was precisely the justification used both by the Roman emperors and by modern absolute rulers for their despotic powers, while the former was believed by many Europeans (not unjustifiably) to be the means by which the native slave traders of West Africa had acquired their prisoners. Grotius's theory thus fitted neatly into the actual practices of his time—something for which Jean-Jacques Rousseau was later vehemently to denounce him.

It was these illiberal implications of the Grotian theory which were especially relevant to Hobbes's view of the English political scene in the late 1630s. Hobbes later said that he had developed his political ideas at this time because his native country was 'burning with the questions of the rights of rulers and the duties of subjects, forerunners of an approaching war' (*De Cive*, Preface 19), and indeed some fundamental political issues were being raised in England between 1637 and 1640. For fifty years England's stance in European politics had been as the ally of Holland in its struggle with the Spanish empire (an alliance which had led to the Armada War itself); now Charles I, alarmed by the developing imperial hegemony of his erstwhile ally, was trying to shift England more into the Spanish camp. His alarm was well founded: the Dutch were creating a formidable empire based on commerce and military power, and even under Cromwell the English were to find themselves fighting against them. But public opinion in England during Charles's reign was very unwilling to sanction such a shift, and Charles knew that the military expenditure necessary could not be funded by a parliamentary grant: for a variety of reasons he had been unprepared to summon a Parliament since 1629. So from 1635 onwards he tried to raise money for a new anti-Dutch fleet through 'Ship Money', an ancient and contentious right of the Crown to tax communities specifically in order to pay for a navy.

There was considerable opposition to this tax, and a famous legal case in 1637 ('Hampden's Case') argued out the issues. The Crown claimed both that any sovereign must have the power to raise military forces for the defence of the realm, and that it must be the sole judge of whether a threat to the realm existed; the opposition conceded the first claim, but denied the second, arguing that public opinion, particularly when represented in a Parliament, could also be the judge of whether a threat existed—and manifestly England's security was not endangered by the Dutch. As we shall see, these must have been the 'questions' to which Hobbes was referring—the argument of the *Elements of Law* is particularly well judged as a contribution to the Ship Money debate, on the King's side. In England as on the Continent, the language of 'natural rights' was thus to be used first as a defence of the established authority.

By 1640 opposition to Charles's policies was getting out of hand. The Scots dealt the final blow by raising an army to resist his ecclesiastical programme in their country, and defeating the English army sent against them. The military débâcle forced Charles to call two Parliaments in 1640, first the 'Short' Parliament and then, in November, the famous 'Long' Parliament. It was clear that when the Parliaments met they would turn against the King's ministers; indeed the Long Parliament passed an Act of Attainder against his principal minister, the Earl of Strafford, who was executed in May 1641. Strafford was an old patron of the Earl of Newcastle, and Newcastle's circle obviously felt both the need to come to his support, and fear lest they be caught up in his downfall. There may even have been a move to have Hobbes stand as a candidate for the Short Parliament—a transition from humanism to politics by no means unprecedented (Grotius is an obvious parallel). Though Hobbes was not himself in the end present in the Parliament, he wrote the *Elements of Law* as a kind of brief for the Earl and his supporters to use in the debates. But when the Long Parliament met, Hobbes's dominant emotion was fear that the *Elements of Law* might be used against him in some future prosecution; accordingly, he suddenly fled to France in November 1640, and stayed there until the winter of 1651–2, throughout the bitter campaigns of the English Civil War.

A few days before going, he decided to let his French friends know how his philosophy had developed, and sent Mersenne what may have been a summary of the *Elements of Philosophy*. Mersenne, as requested, sent the critical sections on Descartes on to Descartes himself, who responded extremely coolly to this unknown opponent. On the strength of this summary, Mersenne also persuaded Hobbes to contribute to a set of objections to a work by Descartes (the *Meditations on First Philosophy*), which was to be published alongside the work itself in 1641. Once settled in Paris, Hobbes busied himself getting ready for the publication in Latin of Section Three of the *Elements of Philosophy*, which naturally included much of the material which had appeared in the political chapters of the *Elements of Law*, and which shared with the English work an obvious and immediate relevance to the political situation. He finished the text in November 1641, and it was printed in April 1642 under the title *Section Three of the Elements of Philosophy: The Citizen (De Cive)*. As the title indicates, Hobbes clearly intended to follow it up reasonably quickly with Sections One and Two, but a number of things delayed him.

The first is that he was now daily in touch with French philosophy, and becoming more aware of the complexities of modern physics and metaphysics. From being a critic of Descartes rather outside the Mersenne circle, he was now more of an ally in a common struggle; thus (probably at Mersenne's request) he devoted much time in 1643 to a critique of an anti-Cartesian and anti-Galilean work by another English exile, Thomas White. A summary of this critique appeared the following year in a volume edited by Mersenne; this was the first public appearance of Hobbes's general philosophy, as distinct from his political theory. By 1646 Hobbes could speak quite warmly of Descartes, depicting himself as a kind of under-labourer to him. They eventually met in 1648, shortly before Descartes emigrated to Sweden, where he died in 1650.

The second reason for the delay was Hobbes's new poverty. Like the other Royalist exiles who joined him in Paris as the war increasingly went against the King, he was cut off from his English income—in his case, the income of the Cavendishes from their estates. In 1646 poverty obliged him to accept the post of tutor in mathematics to the Prince of Wales, later Charles II, who had also arrived in Paris (the Prince later described Hobbes as 'the oddest fellow he ever met with'). This job apparently took up a lot of time, and Hobbes claimed that it prevented him from finishing the *Elements of Philosophy*;

he was also paid extremely erratically for his labours. Nevertheless, by May 1646 he had drafted (in English) a lot of what would later appear as Section Two of the *Elements*, and was well on the way to finishing Section One. However, the fact that when he sanctioned a new edition of *De Cive* that year he amended the title simply to *Philosophical Elements of the Citizen*, and thus avoided committing himself to further instalments, may perhaps be an indication of a new sense of realism. The new edition appeared early in 1647 from the Elzevir Press in Amsterdam, a mass-market publishing house, whose imprint set Hobbes firmly before the international audience. The first edition of *De Cive* had been on a very small scale, and not until 1647 was his name known outside his own circle of friends. Hobbes added to the second edition a number of lengthy explanatory footnotes which often illuminate puzzling areas of his argument better than anything else he ever wrote.

In 1647 he was very ill for some months, and was indeed so close to death that he was given the last rites. He was never to be wholly well again, though his remarkable constitution gave him another thirty years of life; from about 1648 he began to exhibit symptoms which modern scholars have thought indicated Parkinson's disease, and he increasingly came to rely on amanuenses rather than write out his manuscripts personally. This, together with the difficulties consequent upon his move back to England in 1651 (see next section), delayed the completion of the *Elements of Philosophy* even more; as a result Section One did not finally appear until 1655, under the title *Matter (De Corpore)*, and Section Two only appeared in 1658 under the title *Man (De Homine)*. The three sections were not printed together in a single volume until the publishers Blaeu of Amsterdam (another mass-market house) produced a collected edition of Hobbes's Latin works in 1668. Hobbes may have mentally slowed down too: both *De Corpore* and *De Homine* were far from satisfactory in many respects, and have never commanded the enthusiastic following of his earlier works. The story of Hobbes's construction of a philosophical system is thus in the end a story of compromise and tiredness:

the freshness of his early ambitions turned to a weary dogma-tism in the printed volumes which eventually appeared.

The life of a heretic

Though his illness in 1647 may have slowed him down, and though it would not have been surprising for someone in the mid-seventeenth century to have died at the age he was then (fifty-nine), it is a remarkable fact that very soon afterwards he was able to compose his most famous work, *Leviathan*, which appeared from an English publisher in April 1651. Hobbes sent instalments of his manuscript for setting in type each week from Paris to London, with proofs being sent back each week in return—an astonishing method of publishing. It was *Leviathan* which quickly gained for Hobbes the reputation of 'the Beast of Malmesbury'—a reputation which he has never altogether lost, and which led to a long period in which he was under threat from men who had once been his friends. They believed that the book was in many ways a repudiation of all that Hobbes had formerly stood for, and in particular a piece of treachery to the cause of royalism in England—a cause which was in need of redoubled support after the execution of Charles I in January 1649. After the restoration of the monarchy in 1660, Hobbes persistently denied these charges, but they were not wholly unfounded.

One indication of this is the fact that a year after Charles's execution, Hobbes's early works began to be pirated by English publishers, anxious to use them to establish a wholly royalist case against the new republican regime, but Hobbes quite clearly and deliberately refused to allow *Leviathan* to be used in this way. Thus the *Elements of Law* was published (in two parts) early in 1650, and an unauthorized translation of *De Cive* was registered by its publisher in November 1650, actually appearing in the shops in March 1651, at about the same time as *Leviathan* itself. These unauthorized publications were read enthusiastically by Royalists; one of them, an old friend of Hobbes called Robert Payne, after finding the *Elements* in an Oxford bookshop and erroneously taking it to be a pirated translation of *De Cive*, wrote to Hobbes in May 1650 urging him to produce an authorized translation.

The answer he received greatly disconcerted him, for Hobbes replied that he already had 'another trifle on hand' in the shape of an English work on politics, almost two-thirds completed, and being translated into French as he wrote it by a friend of his—a translation which has disappeared. This 'trifle' was, of course, *Leviathan*. When Hobbes told Payne what the new work contained, his old friend was even more disconcerted, for he learned that it involved an explicit attack on the Anglican ecclesiastical order and a defence of what was known as 'Independency'. The attack was contained in Parts Three and Four of the book; Parts One and Two were a restatement of Hobbes's psychological and political ideas, and were substantially the same as the earlier versions. What was significant about *Leviathan*, and the reason why Hobbes wrote it, was the argument embedded in the parts of the book which few modern readers have ever read.

To understand Payne's horror, we have to remember that one of the central issues in the Civil War was the status and organization of the Church. After attainting Strafford and repudiating Charles's policies during the 1630s, the Long Parliament had turned its attention to the Church and proposed the abolition of bishops and their replacement by a system of lay commissioners. For Charles and the Royalists, the preservation of the episcopal Church of England was an issue almost as worth fighting over as the question of who should control the army, though it was the latter issue which actually tipped the nation into open war in 1642; for their parliamentary opponents the reconstruction of the Church was equally important. In 1643 the King looked close to winning the war through his control of the coalfields of north-eastern England, which cut off the energy supplies of London; in order to break this control, Parliament needed to bring the Scots into the war, but the Scots were prepared to come in only if the English agreed to introduce a Presbyterian system of church government, in which clergymen and bodies of lay elders exercised a formidable moral and religious control over the population and over the institutions of the State.

From 1644 until 1649 Parliament was formally committed to such a system, but many English parliamentarians feared it as much as they feared the disciplines of episcopacy. What they wanted was something more like the practice in parts of New England, in which congregations were relatively independent in doctrinal and disciplinary matters, and the State exercised only a loose, supervisory role. Cromwell and the soldiers under him came to represent this Independency, and their military triumph against both the King and, later, the Scots ensured that it was their vision of church government which would prevail in the new republic.

Given this background, it is easy to see why Payne was horrified, for Hobbes was endorsing precisely the principles held by the men who had executed the King. From the time when they came to know what *Leviathan* contained, his old Royalist friends would have nothing more to do with him, and began to accuse him of 'atheism', 'heresy', and 'treachery'—accusations which, it must be stressed, were only rarely levelled at him on account of his earlier works. Even Clarendon, minister to both Charles I and Charles II, admired the *Elements of Law* and *De Cive*, though he too was repelled by *Leviathan*.

Furthermore, Hobbes was not content merely to defend a particular system of church government. When the book was finally published, his former friends were shocked to discover that it also contained what one of them described as 'a farrago of Christian atheism'—a most idiosyncratic version of Christian theology designed to fit in with a materialist philosophy. Though his materialism had never been concealed, and was particularly obvious in his published objections to Descartes's *Meditations*, it had never been so gratuitously offensive to orthodox theology as it was presented in *Leviathan*. The very title of the book was chilling: it was a reference to chapter 41 of the Book of Job in the Bible, in which the 'leviathan' (or sea monster) is described in terms of his absolute and terrifying power—'upon earth there is not his like, who is made without fear'. This was the State as depicted by Hobbes, with absolute power even over God's servants such as Job. The message was rubbed in still more by an astonishing title page (probably

29

designed by the artist Wenceslas Hollar) in which a giant figure composed entirely of a mass of smaller figures is shown looming, sword and crozier in hand, over a settled countryside.

Hobbes quite clearly intended *Leviathan* to be offensive to contemporary, particularly Anglican, sensibilities; he even added a 'Review and Conclusion' in which he explicitly aligned his book with the recent pamphlet literature in England defending the new regime on the basis of its actual possession of power. Why, then, did Hobbes write it? Payne's explanation was that he had been offended in some way by the Anglican clergy gathered at the exile court in Paris, and there may have been something in that. Certainly, Hobbes seems to have been a constant source of irritation to them. This irritation found a relatively honourable expression in a controversy between Hobbes and Bishop John Bramhall in 1645 over free will and determinism, but it may have had a less honourable side— Hobbes seems to have thought that the machinations of the clergy kept him from receiving the full payment for his work as the Prince's tutor.

But we must also remember that the ecclesiastical regime put into place by the new republic after 1649 was very close to what Hobbes seems to have wanted on general grounds, and which he may well have enthusiastically preferred to traditional episcopacy. This is because, like almost all the most interesting seventeenth-century political theorists (including Grotius and Locke), he seems to have feared the moral and intellectual disciplines of Presbyterian Calvinism far more than anything else. It was the Calvinists of Holland who drove Grotius into exile, and who seemed to be a threat to modern sceptical and post-sceptical philosophy; for their opponents, episcopacy was useful as a bulwark against Presbyterianism, but it had a disciplinary structure of its own which might one day be used against philosophy. The relatively tolerant and lay-influenced episcopacy of England in the 1630s was not necessarily to be relied on. But a system of Independency had no general ecclesiastical discipline: all was made free within a structure imposed purely by the State. As we shall see, this corresponded precisely to what Hobbes deeply desired, but which he had presumably thought impossible until 1649.

Indeed, as early as September of that year he told Gassendi that he was inclined to go back to England, and at the end of 1651 (after presenting Charles II with a manuscript copy of *Leviathan*) he slipped across the Channel, never to return to France. The Earl of Devonshire had 'compounded' for some of his estate earlier in the year (that is, had paid the government a lump sum in return for repossessing land of which he had been deprived for supporting the King), and was thus able to pay Hobbes a stipend again; in 1653 Hobbes moved back into his old way of life, living mainly at Devonshire House in London.

His life under the Commonwealth and, later, the Protectorate of Cromwell, was relatively untroubled. He had various friends and supporters under the new regime, of whom perhaps the most interesting was John Selden, who was in many ways the closest English equivalent to Grotius—a lawyer and political theorist who had eagerly taken up the Grotian theory of a minimalist, post-sceptical morality, and who had always been a dedicated opponent of ecclesiastical authority and discipline. Though in the 1620s he had led the parliamentary opposition to the Crown, and to many of Hobbes's friends, in the 1630s he mixed with men like Clarendon and written in defence of the anti-Dutch policies of Charles I. But after being elected to the Long Parliament he committed himself to Parliament's cause during the Civil War, largely because he always believed that he and his friends could eventually secure the kind of ecclesiastical settlement they wanted, with the Church firmly under state control—and so it proved. Many of the leading politicians under both the Commonwealth and the Protectorate admired him; John Milton praised him, and Cromwell at one point considered asking him to write a new constitution for England. Though he and Hobbes did not meet until Hobbes sent him a complimentary copy of *Leviathan*, Hobbes had long respected his work, and he is almost the only person mentioned without cavil in *Leviathan*. Hobbes was allegedly present at his death-bed in 1654, and urged him not to see a priest, remarking (according to Aubrey), 'Will you that have wrote like a man, now dye like a woman?'

But though men like Selden were in power, and Presbyterianism had not triumphed, it had also not conclusively been defeated; some clergymen still wanted to see a national Presbyterian church. Moreover, there were still spokesmen for traditional episcopacy to be found. During the 1650s Hobbes found himself drawn into confrontations with both groups. Against the latter, he published the papers exchanged between himself and Bramhall ten years earlier, to which Bramhall replied with a defence of his own position which went well beyond sober philosophizing.

Much more important, however, was his confrontation with the Presbyterians. This took the form of participating in the struggle between Independents and Presbyterians at Oxford during the middle years of the decade, an involvement which took two forms. On the one hand, he engaged in an acrimonious controversy with a prominent Oxford Presbyterian, John Wallis; this arose from Wallis's objections to some of Hobbes's geometrical arguments in *De Corpore* but quickly spread to cover (in the words of the title of one of Hobbes's contributions) 'the Absurd Geometry, Rural Language, Scottish Church-Politicks and Barbarismes of John Wallis'—a fine catalogue of everything Hobbes detested most. On the other, he provided aid and advice to the Independents at Oxford fighting against men such as Wallis, a group which ranged from a young don called Henry Stubbe (who began to translate *Leviathan* into Latin) to the Vice-chancellor himself, an Independent who had been put into place by the republican government.

The weight of the English political establishment at this time was on Hobbes's side. This was not to be true, however, after the Restoration in 1660. When the republic collapsed in internal feuding after Cromwell's death, it was a hastily constructed coalition of Hobbes's adversaries—the Presbyterians and Anglicans—which paved the way for the return of the King. They were duly rewarded with the establishment of a Presbyterian regime in Scotland and the restoration of the Anglican order in England, in which dissenters were penalized in a variety of ways. Moreover, the men who returned to power from exile with Charles II were in many cases men who had known and admired Hobbes before the war, but now detested him for his apparent treachery. The most spectacular instances of this were two of the principal ministers in the new government, Edward Hyde, Earl of Clarendon, and Gilbert Sheldon, Bishop of London 1660–3 and Archbishop of Canterbury 1663–77. Both men saw themselves as heirs to the Anglican royalism of the late 1630s, which they took Hobbes too to have endorsed at the time; in his autobiography Clarendon depicted the Anglican culture of that age in his idyllic portrayal of the circle of friends who met at Lord Falkland's house at Great Tew in the years before the Civil War, a circle which included Sheldon and many other former friends of Hobbes. They wished now to reinstate the values of Great Tew, and to punish Hobbes for his repudiation of them.

On the other hand, neither Clarendon nor Sheldon had unquestionable power within the new regime. The King himself was by no means a committed Anglican (indeed, he became a secret convert to Roman Catholicism), and many of his courtiers and advisers were either rather raffish libertines or survivors from the Protectorate, neither of which groups were particularly wedded to Clarendon's vision, and both of which were prepared to allow more toleration to dissenters. Hobbes's 'atheism' or 'heresy' in fact became an issue in the struggle within the government between these various figures, which culminated in the impeachment and exile of Clarendon in November 1667. This was because Clarendon repeatedly accused his tolerationist opponents of atheism or profanity, and in October 1666 allowed a Bill to be introduced into the Commons which would for the first time since the Reformation have made Christian heresy a criminal offence. The Commons committee considering the Bill was specifically empowered to gather information about the atheistical implications of *Leviathan*.

Fortunately for *Leviathan's* 78-year-old author, the Bill failed in the Lords despite the efforts of the bishops, and a second attempt to introduce it the following year also failed—though it kept being reintroduced (in 1674, 1675, and 1680). From 1666 until his death Hobbes was therefore faced by the frightening prospect of being either imprisoned or forced into exile for his beliefs. It must have seemed like a replay of 1640, when he fled to France to avoid the hostility of the House of Commons. The threat of official sanctions against him persisted for some time: in March 1668 a Fellow of Corpus Christi College, Cambridge, named Daniel Scargill was deprived of his fellowship for, as his recantation in 1669 put it, 'professing that I gloried to be an *Hobbist* and an *Atheist*'.

These terrifying experiences coloured the rest of Hobbes's life, and drove him to a last burst of composition in order to vindicate himself. He had been told that nothing by him in English would be licensed by the English censors; but in 1668 he published (in the Blaeu edition of his collected Latin works) a translation into Latin of *Leviathan* with an appendix defending his materialism and insisting that under English law there could be no punishment for heresy. He also butchered the sections of the book concerned with ecclesiastical government, dropping his former defence of Independency. At the same time he drafted six works in English, though none were published in his lifetime.

The first was *A dialogue between a philosopher and a student of the common laws of England*, which Hobbes probably wrote in 1666; the second was entitled *An Historical narration concerning heresy, and the punishment thereof*, which he composed in 1668; the third was a new reply to Bramhall (also 1668), and the fourth (which has disappeared) was a comment by Hobbes on the Scargill affair. At some point before the end of 1670 he also composed *Behemoth; or, the Long Parliament*, while the last English manuscript which we know about was a short note on heresy discovered at Chatsworth in 1968. In addition, he is likely to have written during these years his Latin verse *Historia Ecclesiastica*, which is also largely concerned with the theme of heresy.

Heresy is the central theme of all these works: even *Behemoth*, though in form a history of the Civil War, begins with an account of the history of persecution for heresy and then proceeds to argue that it was the evil desire for intellectual control on the part of the Calvinist clergy which precipitated the war. Cromwell is treated with considerable respect, and the restoration of Anglicanism under Clarendon is not even mentioned; in a way, the Restoration is depicted as the culmination of the lay attack on Presbyterian Calvinism begun during the war. Moreover, the point of the first English work, the *Dialogue of the common laws*, was to show that on Hobbes's interpretation of the source of English law, there could be no valid actions against anyone for heresy. In the process, however, he provided some fine general discussions of the nature of law in general and the English common law in particular, which have made the work deservedly popular with modern readers. It is also worth remarking that many of Hobbes's post-Restoration works are couched in the form of dialogues, an interesting return to a deeply humanist practice (though Wallis, for one, complained that they were dialogues 'between Thomas and Hobbes').

Neither the Earl of Devonshire nor the Earl of Newcastle could be of much use to Hobbes in this crisis, since both had substantially retired from public life after the Restoration. He did, however, find a patron who could assist him; this was Henry Bennet, Earl of Arlington, who was one of Clarendon's leading opponents, and whom Hobbes may have met when he was attached to the exiled court. Like the King, Arlington was more sympathetic to Catholicism than to Anglicanism, and favoured loosening the restrictions on dissenters of all kinds; he helped Hobbes to evade the wrath of the Commons in 1666–7, and provided some helpful comments on the *Historical narration concerning heresy* (though he was unable to get it passed by the censors). *Behemoth* was dedicated to him, as was one of Hobbes's polemical works on geometry; it was probably through his influence that Hobbes was introduced to the Grand Duke Cosimo di Medici of Tuscany on the Grand Duke's state visit in 1669. The Grand Duke was so impressed that he took back with him copies of Hobbes's works and a portrait of the philosopher to hang in the Medici collections in Florence.

Arlington was a particularly useful patron as, after Clarendon's fall, he was one of the five ministers who formed a new government (known after their initials as the Cabal—Clifford, Arlington, Buckingham, Ashley Cooper, and Lauderdale). They came to power with the avowed aim of promoting religious toleration or comprehension: that is, either an established Anglican church but with civil rights for non-Anglican churches, or a national church which contained within itself a wide range of dissenting opinions; during their years in office (which lasted roughly until 1674) they attracted about themselves a number of advisers committed to the same project.

Some of the advisers were old friends of Selden—two lawyers, John Vaughan and Matthew Hale, who were given high legal office and consulted on legal matters concerning toleration, were Selden's executors. Vaughan read Hobbes's *Dialogue of the common laws* in manuscript, and liked it; Hale also read it, and though he wrote a critique of it he too was sympathetic to some of its basic points. Another adviser was John Locke; he was extremely close at this time to Ashley Cooper, from 1672 the Earl of Shaftesbury. He drafted papers and speeches on toleration for his master, at the same time as Hobbes was writing papers on heresy for Arlington—a singular conjunction of the two great seventeenth-century English philosophers working in a common cause. We do not know if they met—though in 1673 Hobbes's friend John Aubrey wrote to Locke asking him to look at the manuscripts about heresy which Hobbes had drafted (particularly the *Dialogue of the common laws* and *Behemoth*), and observing that 'the old gent. is still strangely vigorous. If you see him (which he would take kindly) pray my service to him.'

The conjunction of Hobbes and Locke should alert us to the fact that the Cabal's policies cut across the conventional categories of English politics. They sought toleration, but they sought it by and large against the opposition of an Anglican and anti-tolerationist Parliament, which (for example) in 1673 passed the Test Act, requiring any holder of civil or military office to be a member of the Church of England. The Cabal ministers were thus prepared to elevate monarchical power, if by doing so they undermined the power of the Church; in many ways this was the keynote of 'enlightened despotism', as the term came to be employed to describe the activities of the liberal but despotic rulers of eighteenth-century Europe such as Catherine the Great of Russia. Locke's papers for Shaftesbury at this time wholly endorse such an approach, and it was of course very close to what Hobbes had always wanted. Indeed, one might say that throughout the seventeenth century in England there was an Anglican, Tory majority in the country, and anyone who wanted toleration would be pretty sceptical about Parliaments; Locke, even in his later and more revolutionary phase, remained unenamoured of full parliamentary sovereignty.

But the last of the Cabal ministers fell in 1674 in the face of entrenched Anglicanism and a monarch unwilling in the end to offend the Tory, Anglican order. No long-term change in the ecclesiastical settlement had been achieved, and dissent had only been tolerated through the issue by Charles of declarations of indulgence—acts of pure and arbitrary royal power. By 1675 the resurgent anti-tolerationists were seeking to extend the Test Act by enforcing an oath on all office-holders binding them not to 'endeavour the alteration of the Government either in Church or State'. At this point Locke was driven into exile, and into a new and radical commitment to armed revolution in defence of religious pluralism; but here his path and Hobbes's diverged. The 'old gent.' was eighty-seven in 1675, and no longer particularly frightened for his personal safety; he had returned to his first love, translation, and in 1674 completed an English version of the *Iliad* and *Odyssey*. But he did leave London in 1675, and spent the rest of his life in the country at Hardwick; Cavendish family tradition later held that he also started going to church and taking communion, but always turned his back on the sermon.

Nevertheless, he had one last contribution to make to political debate, though only within the Devonshire household. At the end of 1678 the balance of power in London swung once more against the Anglicans, and the Earl of Danby, their spokesman, was impeached. A move was started to have

Charles's younger brother and heir apparent, James Duke of York, excluded from the succession; this was ostensibly because he was an avowed Catholic, but in reality because Charles's illegitimate son, the Duke of Monmouth (who would, the exclusionists hoped, become his heir), looked like an ideal monarch for the dissenting interest. The issue of 'exclusion' was to dominate English politics until Charles's death in 1685, and it was as a contribution to the debates about it that Locke wrote his famous *Two Treatises of Government*. The Earl of Devonshire's eldest son, Lord Cavendish, who sat in the Parliament of 1675–9, was a keen member of the anti-Danby faction, and a moderate supporter of exclusion; he later became a prominent Whig and the first Duke of Devonshire, having helped to engineer the Revolution of 1688. How far Hobbes would have approved of his later conduct it is hard to say; but he did sketch out, almost certainly for Lord Cavendish's use, some thoughts on the principle of exclusion which must date from early 1679. He concluded that a sovereign could perfectly legitimately exclude his natural heir from succession, but could not be *forced* to do so by his subjects—a position which may well have corresponded quite closely with Cavendish's at the time, given that he was hoping that Charles would agree to the exclusion of the Duke of York.

This was to be Hobbes's last service for the family he had served through four generations, and which now treated him as a cross between a servant and an honoured guest. His standing with them in his old age is vividly illustrated by a memoir compiled from family reminiscences in 1708, in which it was recorded, for example, that after breakfast each day he 'went around the Lodgings to wait upon [i.e. to greet] the Earl, the Countess and the Children, and any considerable Strangers, paying some short Addresses to all of them. He kept these Rounds till about 12 a Clock, when he had a little Dinner provided for him, which he eat always by himself without Ceremony'. In October 1679 he fell ill, and on 3 December he died at Hardwick. A variety of rumours circulated about his state of mind on his deathbed—always a keen source of interest where a suspected atheist was concerned. It is clear that he did not see a priest nor take the sacrament, though his friends explained this by the suddenness of his final seizure; there is also good evidence of his having remarked bleakly that 'he was 91 years finding a hole to go out of this world, and at length found it'. The inscription over his tomb in the parish church of Ault Hucknall, near Hardwick, which he composed himself, is wholly and proudly secular. He allegedly considered seriously but finally rejected the epitaph 'This is the true philosopher's stone'—which, a clerical critic observed, would have had 'as much Religion in it, as that which now remains'. He seems in fact to have died much as he had lived, a witty and sceptical humanist.

II Hobbes's work

Science

As we saw in Part I, there are good grounds for supposing that Hobbes began his philosophical enquiries in the late 1630s because he was intrigued by the philosophical problems raised by modern natural science, and particularly by the possibility of replacing late Renaissance scepticism with a philosophy accommodated to the ideas (above all) of Galileo. The crucial idea, as we also saw, was simply to treat what is perceived by man—the images and so on which are immediately apparent to an internal observer—as bearing no relationship of *verisimilitude* to the external world. Man is effectively a prisoner within the cell of his own mind, and has no idea what in reality lies outside his prison walls. Like Descartes and Gassendi, Hobbes had come to believe this by 1637, and was then spurred on by Descartes's hyper-scepticism into working out a new theory as to what kind of things must lie beyond the prison. This new theory was the basis of the metaphysics and physics which occupied him down to the publication of *De Corpore* in 1655 and *De Homine* in 1658.

Its fundamental propositions hardly altered during that time, and may be found (often expressed in virtually the same words) in his works from the *Elements of Law* and the first draft of the *Elements of Philosophy*, through the *Critique of Thomas White* and *Leviathan* itself, down to the final publication of the *Elements of Philosophy*. Having established the prevalence of optical illusion, and the impossibility of believing that what we think we see, such as colour, is *really* a property of an external object, Hobbes asserted (in the words of the *Elements of Law*, which is often the most accessible statement of his general philosophy) that

> whatsoever accidents or qualities our senses make us think there be in the world, they are not there, but are seemings

and apparitions only. The things that really are in the world without us, are those motions by which these seemings are caused. And this is the great deception of sense, which also is by sense to be corrected. For as sense telleth me, when I see directly, that the colour seemeth to be in the object; so also sense telleth me, when I see by reflection, that colour is not in the object. (I.2.10)

In other words, the senses themselves give us evidence of the unreality of what they present to us as real: we have only to reflect on the implications of such things as a reflected image to realize that seeing something does not in itself give us any grounds for supposing that the thing seen is *really* in the place it appears to be or has the properties which we think it has.

But the important work in this passage is done by the second sentence, which expresses Hobbes's conviction that there is actually something outside us (against Descartes's doubt), and that it consists of 'motions'. The *Elements of Law* and his other ethical and political works merely assume this to be so, but in the first section of the *Elements of Philosophy* Hobbes presents an argument against what is in effect the Cartesian sceptic. Though the original draft of the first section is lost, notes on various early versions survive, and it was clearly drawn on by Hobbes in his Objections to Descartes's *Meditations* of 1641 and his *Critique of Thomas White* in 1643; it is also referred to in the surviving early version of Section Two. The argument began in a wholly Cartesian manner by imagining, in the words of what is probably the earliest set of notes,

the world annihilated except one man to whom there would remain ideas and images of all the things he had seen, or perceived by his other senses . . .: all which though in truth they would be only ideas and phantasms internally happening and falling to the imaginant himself, nevertheless they would appear as if they were external and not depending upon the power or virtue of the mind.

This technique of using the image of a mind left floating in a wholly empty universe was one which Hobbes was still using when he finally published Section One as *De Corpore* in 1655.

The question which Hobbes then put to himself was the same one which Descartes had put about his disengaged mind: what could such a man think, and how could he come to *know* anything about the universe in which he found himself, and about its history (including the fact, as Hobbes believed it to be, that the man's own thoughts must have been the product of a physical process within the universe prior to the annihilation of everything but himself)?

Hobbes's answer went in essence as follows. First, it would be perfectly possible for the man to have a complete language, referring to everything which he believed to exist in the same way as our languages refer to what we think exists outside us. Everything which it is possible for us to think or reason about would be possible for him too, since the actual existence of anything which is the object of our thinking is irrelevant. A language is simply a formal system whose relationship to reality is puzzling and contentious; but it is the only tool we have to *reason* with. Hobbes consistently used the analogy of counting to explain what he meant by reasoning. Just as effective counting consists in understanding the rules of a formal system (the natural numbers) which may not have any precise relationship to reality, so effective reasoning consists in understanding the meanings of words within the system of language without necessarily having any clear belief about what they refer to. As Hobbes said in a famous phrase from *Leviathan*, 'words are wise mens counters, they do but reckon by them: but they are the mony of fooles' (p. 106)—for fools believe words to have some real value.

He believed the same to be true of the only fully satisfactory example of a system of reasoning yet produced, namely Euclidean geometry. The method of exposition employed by Euclid and his successors was to define precisely the meaning of terms such as 'line' and 'point', and to draw conclusions (allegedly) strictly from these definitions. The system was thus self-contained and conventional, as Hobbes believed an ideal language to be. And, like a language, assessing its relationship to reality required some further theory; in the case of geometry, Hobbes argued that the Euclidean definitions were in fact met by the behaviour of a moving body, the *direction* of whose movement could be thought of as a line without breadth (a line without breadth being the famous, and famously puzzling, definition of a line employed by Euclid). Hobbes believed that this approach met the sceptical objections which had been advanced even to geometry in antiquity; he also believed that it could solve the famous 'impossible' problems such as squaring the circle, whose alleged impossibility seemed to him, reasonably enough, to be part of the sceptics' case. He wasted many years in futile attempts to solve these puzzles, his 'theorems' being treated with contempt by men like Wallis, who were better mathematicians but worse philosophers.

Hobbes's solipsist alone in the universe would thus be able to talk and think; he would even have available to him the whole of geometry. But what he would think would be rather different from the musings of Descartes's sceptic. First of all, while Hobbes accepted the validity of the proposition *I think, therefore I am* (acknowledging as much in his Objections to Descartes's *Meditations*), he did not conclude from this that his solipsist would come up with Descartes's idea of a mind separate from its own perceptions and witnessing them like an observer witnesses the events outside him—the famous Cartesian 'Ego'. Instead, he insisted that the solipsist would think of himself just *as* the train of perceptions, because he could not perceive anything (so to speak) doing the thinking.

> Although someone may think that he *was* thinking (for this thought is simply an act of remembering), it is quite impossible for him to think that he *is* thinking, or to know that he is knowing. For then an infinite chain of questions would arise: How do you know that you know that you know . . .? (2nd Objection)

The self in this sense is imaginary, simply a construct arising from our inability to conceive of thinking without a thinker to *do* it.

Second, the perceptions which flit across the solipsist's mind (just as they flit continuously across our minds) would give him the ideas of space and time, but he would, Hobbes argued, come to see that space and time are *also* imaginary. The proposition that space and time are imaginary might seem astonishing, but Hobbes's point was that no one has ever had direct experience of them: they are constructs or deductions from what we do directly experience. Space cannot really be apprehended except as something which a body occupies (even the emptiness of inter-stellar space, he might have said, we really think of as full of something—the kind of black, transparent medium in which planets and spaceships move, and which it is impossible actually to picture as boundless). Similarly time is a 'phantasm of motion': we can directly experience moving objects, but not that they are moving 'in' time any more than that they are moving 'in' space.

So far, the solipsist is in no better position than the Cartesian sceptic, for he is still incapable of coming to any conclusions about what is really to be found in an external universe. He knows what objects in space and time would be, but he does not yet know whether everything he perceives is imaginary or not. In some ways his position is even worse, because he even thinks of his own self as imaginary. It is a vertiginous and disturbing picture, the metaphysical counterpart of the radically individualist political world Hobbes was to depict. But at this point Hobbes brought a new argument to bear on his dilemma. One thing the solipsist does know is that his own thoughts exhibit *change*: he does not gaze out mentally over an unchanging landscape, but is presented with the same succession of images, sounds, and so on with which we are presented every moment of our lives. And it is natural for the solipsist to ask how this can be: what is it which leads him to have *changing* or *moving* images in front of him? This is a question which Descartes's sceptic had failed to ask; Descartes did in a way depict him as someone contemplating a single image in front of his mind's eye rather than the moving pictures postulated by Hobbes.

Hobbes answered the solipsist's question using a number of metaphysical propositions which played an absolutely vital role in both his physics and his psychological theories. The first and most important one was the proposition that *nothing can move itself*, which he asserted on the basis of what is known in the history of philosophy as the 'principle of sufficient reason'—that is, the principle that there has to be some new feature in a situation to explain some new alteration in it. A body which displayed no other alteration in its condition could not therefore start to move. Hobbes always insisted that self-movement was literally inconceivable.

The second proposition was that nothing could be moved except bodies in space, and the third was that only bodies could move other bodies—there can be no explanations of movement involving 'incorporal substances'. Hobbes again presented these propositions as necessarily true, their falsehood being inconceivable: the first because movement *means* alteration in spatial position, and only bodies occupy space, the second because (in the words of the *Critique*) 'we can conceive of only one efficient cause that sets in motion any body initially at rest: the motion of an adjacent body. As the commencement of motion is the quitting of place, we can see that the only reason why a body leaves its place is that another body standing adjacent replaces the first by moving forward' (fo. 300). This was the central plank of Hobbes's philosophical vessel.

The answer to the solipsist was, then, that there must be, or have been, some material object outside himself which was causing him to have the perceptions which he had. He could not be causing them himself, since nothing can cause its own alterations, and he has no 'self' other than the train of perceptions. And the thing outside him must be *material*, since nothing else could produce a change in anything.

But this is actually as far as Hobbes ever went, or intended to go, in answering the solipsist. Everything else—that is, the actual character of the external world and of our relationship to it—must remain conjectural or hypothetical, though some hypotheses are better than others. I will consider two examples of such hypotheses, each of peculiar importance within Hobbes's theory. The first, which also tells us a lot about Hobbes's thinking about *reasoning*, concerns the central Cartesian puzzle about dreaming. While the Cartesian sceptic was particularly troubled by the doubt that everything which we experience while (apparently) awake might merely be a dream, the Hobbesian solipsist was not one bit troubled by his identical fear. As Hobbes said in the *Elements of Law*, it is not

> impossible for a man to be so far deceived, as when his dream is past, to think it real: for if he dream of such things as are ordinarily in his mind, and in such order as he useth to do waking, and withal that he laid him down to sleep in the place where he findeth himself when he awaketh (all which may happen) I know no *criterion* or mark by which he can discern whether it were a dream or not . . . (I.3.10)

But from Hobbes's point of view that simply did not matter: our thoughts while asleep are *caused* in exactly the same way as our thoughts while awake, that is to say, by the bombardment of external objects upon our senses and by the resonances set up inside our brain by the bombardment; and it may well be that we are asleep and dreaming, or that the world outside ourselves no longer exists.

There are, however, some lower-level considerations which might in general recommend to us the hypothesis that we have been dreaming and are now awake. The principal one, which Hobbes made much of in his discussions of human psychology, is that there are obvious differences between an *ordered* and a *disordered* train of thought. As an example of the latter, Hobbes (with considerable insight into the mind of the mentally disturbed) depicted someone running from one thought to another via a combination of word associations or puns, and the association of objects. Dreams, he believed, normally exhibited a comparable disorder. On the other hand, waking, conscious, and rational thought was characteristically distinguished by a purposive sequencing of ideas: rather than merely being the victim of random associations, the thinker considered a series of images in order to get something he wanted or was interested in. If we are at present running through such a sequence, then we can say we are 'awake' (while leaving open the logical possibility that we are asleep). His picture of rational or ordered thought seems in fact to have been like the modern notion of a properly organized computer program: we can distinguish between a case where the program is functioning smoothly, and the machine is thereby doing something effectively, and a case where there is some malfunction. But in either case the computer remains a machine, and the difference between the cases is a purely formal one.

Hobbes was indeed always at pains to stress that this distinction did not imply that the rational thinker was 'free' in some metaphysical sense to order his thoughts as he wished. Hobbes's ideas about free will and determinism were among the most puzzling and contentious of his views for his contemporaries (witness his prolonged debate with Bishop Bramhall), and they have continued to attract considerable argument. Obviously, his commitment to the propositions that there is no 'self' independent of the activity of thinking, and that nothing moves itself, immediately ruled out any orthodox notion of free will: there was nothing that could *be* free and alter an agent's perceptions and actions in the orthodox way. 'Freedom' for Hobbes was still a meaningful term, but it meant purely the condition of having no hindrance to the securing of what one wants; the will itself, or the act of wanting, could not be free. The idea of the 'free self' was as imaginary as the idea of the self: 'a wooden top that is lashed by the boys, and runs about sometimes to one wall, sometimes to another, sometimes spinning, sometimes hitting men on the shins, if it were sensible of its own motion, would think it proceeded from its own will, unless it felt what lashed it.' ('The Questions concerning Liberty, Necessity, and Chance'). This metaphysical argument gave an additional purchase to the attack on the traditional humanist notion of civic liberty which, as we shall see, Hobbes undertook in his political works—for if no one can be truly free, there is no point in proclaiming that one can be at liberty only under a certain constitutional regime.

The second example of Hobbes's hypotheses about the physical world which I want to consider is his idea about the nature of *light*. Hobbes was always very proud of his theory of light, holding it and his political theory to be his main contributions to modern thought; as we have seen, optics (the analysis of both the transmission of light and of vision) was a subject to which he constantly returned. Descartes's theory of light was once again the target. Descartes believed that the universe was filled with some substance to which any light source applied pressure. This pressure was felt by the eye, which interpreted it very sensitively as a visible emanation from the source. The transmission of light was thus like the transmission of a movement from one end of a stick to the other, and vision was in principle the same as the activity of a blind man feeling his way along a street with his stick. Hobbes never denied that such a theory fitted his metaphysical criteria for a good scientific theory: it involved, after all, purely mechanical effects brought about by material objects. But he once again used a variety of lower-level considerations to suggest a different hypothesis (at least in his works prior to 1645), which later scientists regarded as a major idea.

This different hypothesis was that a light source such as the sun is like the human heart (or indeed any pump), alternately expanding and contracting and sending pulses of matter out towards an observer. For this image Hobbes drew explicitly on the work of William Harvey, whose discovery of the circulation of the blood had been announced in a book published in 1628. Hobbes was greatly impressed by Harvey, whose vision of the human body as constantly in motion corresponded so well with his own metaphysics. The analogy with the circulation of the blood was, however, only partial, since light does not form a closed and circulating system, and Hobbes was always troubled by the problem of how a light source could dilate. To explain this, he insisted (against Descartes) in these early works that a vacuum must be possible, so that a dilating object simply became less dense by virtue of tiny vacuums springing up in its interstices; but he gradually came to be persuaded by experimental evidence and by the force of Descartes's arguments that a vacuum is impossible. The consequence was that he had to abandon his early theory of light, and in *De Corpore* it is replaced by a much less persuasive one (in which a luminous body actually has to move its position in space to produce the sensation of light). Eighteenth- and nineteenth-century scientists, who had only a vague knowledge of Hobbes's early works, had laboriously to reinvent the hypothesis that light is emitted in a pulse-like motion; in this respect Hobbes's instinct for what a good scientific explanation might be was to be shared later by many practising scientists.

Not that Hobbes would have been particularly impressed by this fact. The appearance in his lifetime of something resembling the practice of modern science, notably in the form of what Robert Boyle and the early members of the Royal Society were up to, attracted from him nothing but derision (expressed pungently in his Latin *Physical dialogue on the nature of air* of 1661, one of the contributions to his long controversy with Wallis and Wallis's supporters, and addressed especially to Boyle). The reason for his contempt was twofold. The first was that for political reasons (which I shall outline later) he mistrusted any privileged body of intellectuals who might come to have some kind of independent ideological authority over their fellow citizens—and presciently he saw that modern scientists might form just such a new priesthood.

The second reason was that he mistrusted any great reliance on experimental evidence to prove the truth or falsehood of scientific theories. As he said in the *Elements of Law* (I.4.10), 'experience concludeth nothing universally'. Every experiment produces information about how human beings perceive their world, and nothing more; consequently, a scientist has to be extremely careful about his interpretation of any experimental results, and must constantly put them in the context of his theory of perception, which in turn must be set in the context of a general metaphysical theory. Unless these backing theories were correct, the experiment could tell the scientist little of use. As an example of fallacious reasoning, he used the proudest claim made by Robert Boyle, that he had succeeded in producing an artificial vacuum by pumping all the air out of a large glass container, in which various experiments could then be performed. As Hobbes observed, all Boyle should in fact have claimed was that he had managed to pump out of his container everything which a pump could extract—and since it remained a wholly open question what sort of thing could *not* be pumped out, it must also remain an open question whether Boyle had in fact produced a vacuum. Hobbes's contempt for experimental machinery of this kind was well expressed in a remark from another work in this controversy, of 1662: 'not every one that brings from beyond seas a new gin [engine], or other jaunty device, is therefore a philosopher. For if you reckon that way, not only apothecaries and gardeners, but many other sorts of workman, will put in for, and get the prize ('Considerations upon the Reputation, Loyalty, Manners, and Religion of Thomas Hobbes').

Despite his contempt for the actual practice of most modern scientists, in many ways Hobbes's philosophy is closer to the assumptions on which modern science rests than any of the competing philosophies on offer in the seventeenth century. It shared with Descartes's the stress on the need to think of the real world as essentially different from how we experience it, and this stress has been characteristic of the most important achievements of the physical sciences—beginning with Galileo pointing out that the experience of someone on the earth itself could not determine whether the earth was rotating, and ending with the utterly unimaginable postulates of modern theoretical physics about the objects which really make up the material universe. But, unlike Descartes, Hobbes was able to make sense of a material world outside our minds without bringing in elaborate theological postulates, which fits the secular cast of mind of many modern scientists. It should be said, however, that Hobbes (despite his own pleas) has rarely been seen as the key theoretician of modern science—which illustrates the dubiousness of the notion that there was a historical link between modern science and the process of secularization. Seventeenth- and eighteenth-century scientists in fact disowned the one truly secular philosophy of science on offer to them, preferring instead the elaborate theological speculations in which Newton indulged. In this respect, Hobbes's theory of science represented an exploration of intellectual possibilities which were not to be opened up again for another two hundred years.

Ethics

Just as Hobbes's philosophy of science was in effect designed to validate and explain the traditional sceptical view that our observation of the world is radically contaminated by illusion, so his philosophy of ethics was intended to underwrite the traditional sceptic's moral relativism. It is important to stress here that Hobbes's writings on politics were intended to elucidate broadly *ethical* issues, and that he was not concerned (at least on the face of it) with explaining political behaviour in the supposedly 'value-free' manner of a modern political scientist. The dedicatory letters to both the *Elements of Law* and *De Cive* make this absolutely clear—particularly perhaps the latter, in which Hobbes remarked that 'what deals with figures, is called *Geometry*, with motion, *Physics*, and with natural right, *Morals*: all of them together are *Philosophy*'. The central problem with which he was concerned in the third section of his philosophy was thus not the explanation of human action (that belonged, if anywhere, in Section Two), but the problem of 'natural right'—the existence or non-existence of common ethical standards by which men should live their lives.

As we saw in Part I, the particular kind of humanism which had been fashionable in Hobbes's youth, and which was represented above all by the figures of Montaigne and Lipsius, stressed the sheer multiplicity of human beliefs and customs and threw up its hands in despair at the prospect of finding any common moral denominator. All that it was safe to say of human beings, these humanists came to believe, was that they are primarily concerned with preserving themselves in a dangerous world—and one made doubly dangerous by the presence of competing ideologies. This impulse to self-preservation, however, was not itself a moral matter. As we also saw in Part I, Hugo Grotius proposed what is in retrospect (like most good ideas) an obvious twist to this argument, namely that self-preservation *is* a moral principle: it is the foundational 'natural right' upon which all known moralities and codes of social behaviour must have been constructed. But it is balanced by a fundamental duty or 'natural law' to abstain from harming other people except where our own preservation is at stake.

Grotius's idea was that there must be a kind of equilibrium of permitted violence for any society to survive. If *too little* violence were permitted—that is, if people were not allowed to defend themselves when wantonly attacked—then a few aggressive individuals would destroy the rest. If *too much* violence were permitted—if people were allowed to attack other members of the society for whatever reasons they themselves thought fit—then this too would wreck the possibility of social life. So whatever the laws and customs of a society (and Grotius was as fully conscious as any earlier relativist of the enormous moral divergences between societies), they must in part be designed to protect this equilibrium of violence. Beyond this common core, however, societies could differ extravagantly in their laws, and anything which was accepted as law in a particular society would be immune to moral criticism coming from someone outside the society.

This was the most up-to-date and appealing moral theory on offer when Hobbes began to write the ethical section of his *Elements of Philsophy*, and it is not surprising that we constantly find echoes of Grotius in his works. It should be said that Grotius is virtually never referred to by *name*; but he shares that characteristic with almost all other philosophers, both past and contemporary—Hobbes being extremely reluctant to locate his own ideas in any familiar intellectual context. Hobbes's first task was to show that the relativist idea was correct, and could be explained by his own philosophy of science; he then had to show that something like the Grotian theory also followed from his fundamental principles—though he introduced into it a new sceptical twist, comparable perhaps to the hyperbolical doubt which Descartes had introduced in the course of his refutation of scepticism, and his answer to this new doubt pushed his political conclusions some way away from Grotius's.

The relativist idea was pungently expressed by Hobbes in the *Elements of Law*:

Every man, for his own part, calleth that which pleaseth, and is delightful to himself, GOOD; and that EVIL which displeaseth him: insomuch that while every man differeth from other in constitution, they differ also one from another concerning the common distinction of good and evil. Nor is there any such thing as ἀγαθὸν ἁπλῶς [*agathon haplos*], that is to say, simply good. For even the goodness which we attribute to God Almighty, is his goodness to us. And as we call good and evil the things that please and displease us; so call we goodness and badness, the qualities of powers whereby they do it. (I.7.3)

Hobbes, in other words, treated *moral* terms in exactly the same way as he had treated colour terms: though common language and common sense might lead us to think that something is really and objectively good, in the same way as we might think something is really and objectively red, in fact such ideas are illusions or fantasies, features of the inside of our heads only. The sensation of colour is to be understood, as we have seen, as what it feels like to come under the influence of something in the external world which is not itself a colour, but a pulse of light impinging on our eyes; similarly, moral approval or disapproval are to be understood as feelings engendered by the impact of something external on the system of passions and wants which make up the human emotive psychology.

That there is such a system, Hobbes not unnaturally took for granted, regarding it as a matter of direct introspective observation. He equally took it for granted that the system must function in accordance with the general metaphysical principles he had laid down for all scientific explanation—that is, it must take the form of what we might call a *ballistical* system, in which moving bodies interact in various ways. But the specific theory he put forward was, like his optics, a *theory* only, though he claimed that it was superior to all other hypotheses available.

For it, he drew once again on Harvey's discovery of the circulation of the blood, and proposed that it was one part of a complicated system involving 'animal' and 'vital' spirits. To understand this, we have to remember that even school-children nowadays are incomparably better equipped to talk about basic chemistry than the most highly educated intellectual of Stuart England. We possess, for example, the absolutely familiar and useful term 'gas' to describe a particular state in which matter can be found; but the word was only invented by a Flemish medical alchemist in Hobbes's lifetime, and was not in common usage for another hundred years. We also have the notion of electrical transmission through fibres, and an awareness that electricity and chemistry are intimately connected; again, no one in Hobbes's time could have had these ideas. So we must not think that he meant by 'spirit' anything particularly mysterious, and especially that he meant something *incorporeal*—Hobbes always insisted, as we have seen, that there could be no such thing.

What he meant was simply that there is some mechanical system in the body whereby sense-perceptions are transmitted to the brain, and that they there cause perturbations to the 'spirits' which link the brain and the heart, and that the consequent perturbations in the heart affect the circulation of the blood—and *in extremis* would cut it off altogether, killing the animal. The different physiological changes during this process are describable in terms of the familiar language of perception and emotion: thus the alterations in the make-up of the brain are *perceptions*, and the alterations in the behaviour of the blood are *passions*. Both kinds of alteration mistakenly lead people to attribute relevant properties to external objects, so that a spider, for example, can seem both 'black' and 'frightening', and perhaps also 'evil', though none of these terms really refers to anything.

Because moral judgements are a matter of feeling as well as perception, it was reasonable for Hobbes to say on the basis of this theory (as he always did) that the description of something as 'good' must be broadly the same as the description of it as 'pleasurable'—for the feeling of moral approbation is in a way a feeling of pleasure at the action in question. But it would also have been reasonable for him to have pointed out that the two feelings are not quite the same, and that the difference between them needs some explanation (a point made later, in effect, by Hume). That he never did, and persisted in holding that 'the good' and 'the pleasurable' were identical, is best seen as the consequence of his immersion in the scepticism of Montaigne's time, with its standard assumption that people take to be 'good' what is in their own interest (or, in the Latin terminology which they employed, and which went back to comparable arguments to be found in Cicero, that what was *honestum* was what was *utile*).

Having insinuated this identity, Hobbes had both stated and explained moral relativism: there were no objective moral properties, but what seemed good was what pleased any individual or was good *for him*. The implicit 'realism' of ordinary moral language, like that of the ordinary language of colour, was therefore a serious error. Hobbes indeed usually treated this error as the major difficulty in the way of a peaceful life, rather than (as is often supposed) viewing the clash of naked self-interest as the fundamental problem in human social existence.

The account of the passions which Hobbes gave, after all, treated them as broadly beneficial: what men feel strongly about or desire strongly is what helps them to survive, and they cannot for long want a state of affairs in which their survival is endangered. Such a view was common ground between Hobbes and many of his contemporaries, including Descartes: all argued that the traditional idea that reason should control the passions was an error, and that (properly understood) our emotions would guide us in the right direction. Men, on Hobbes's account, do not want to harm other men *for the sake of harming them*; they wish for power over them, it is true, but power only to secure their own preservation. The common idea that Hobbes was in some sense 'pessimistic' about human nature is wide of the mark, for his natural men (rather like Grotius's) were in principle stand-offish towards one another rather than inherently belligerent.

But Hobbes did believe that such creatures could not enjoy a decent social existence unless they were capable of using a common moral language to describe their activities. This is simply a deep-rooted assumption in his work, which is never fully justified, but which is constantly implied by the way in which he described the problem of human conflict. In *De Cive*, for example, he observed that

> the desires of men are different, as men differ among themselves in temperament, custom and opinion; we see this in sense-perceptions such as taste, touch or smell, but even more in the common business of life, where what one person *praises*—that is, calls *good*—another will *condemn* and call *evil*. Indeed, often the same man at different times will *praise* and *blame* the same thing. As long as this is the case there will necessarily arise discord and conflict. (III.31)

It was conflict over what to *praise*, or morally to approve, which Hobbes thus isolated as the cause of discord, rather than simple conflict over *wants*. What he was frightened of, it is reasonable to assume, were such things as the Wars of Religion, or other ideological wars; not (say) class wars, in which the clash of wants could more clearly be seen.

The malleability of opinion by outside forces was part of this problem: as he said in the passage just quoted, the same man could often believe quite different things, depending on the circumstances. In *Leviathan*, indeed, Hobbes describes the minds of 'the Common-people' as 'like clean paper, fit to receive whatsoever by Publique Authority shall be imprinted in them' unless they had already been 'scribbled over with the opinions of their Doctors' (ch. 30, p. 379). Controlling or combating the pens which could write on this clean paper was crucial, and it was this which led him throughout his work bitterly to condemn the activities of rhetoricians: 'such is the power of eloquence, as many times a man is made to believe thereby, that he sensibly feeleth smart and damage, when he feeleth none, and to enter into rage and indignation, without any cause, than what is in the words and passion of the speaker' (*Elements of Law* II.8.14; see also *De Cive* XII.12). This was despite the fact that he himself, like all humanists, was both fascinated by and very skilled at rhetoric; indeed he wrote a couple of works on the subject to be read by his Cavendish pupils (one was published in 1637). But the power of rhetoric, and of other outside influences on opinion, made the resolution of conflict a doubly difficult affair.

Nevertheless, Hobbes believed that there was a solution to moral conflict. The traditional moralist's response to ethical disagreement had been to hope that sooner or later everyone would come to see the moral *facts* clearly and rationally, but Hobbes of course could not resort to pious hopes of this kind. Instead, he proposed that the route to agreement must lie through *politics*, and this must count as Hobbes's most distinctive contribution to political theory. He put his idea most clearly, and most sceptically, in a passage of the *Elements of Law* where he contrasted a 'state of nature' (by which he meant the condition of men without some proper political organization) with the state of men under a regime of civil laws—a state later writers standardly termed 'civil society', but which Hobbes (though he did sometimes use that expression) more commonly called a 'commonwealth' or, when he wrote in Latin, a *civitas* ('city' or 'state'). This passage contains, I believe, an accurate summary of the whole of Hobbes's theory, and is worth quoting at length.

> In the state of nature, where every man is his own judge, and differeth from other concerning the names and appellations of things, and from those differences arise quarrels, and breach of peace; it was necessary there should be a common measure of all things that might fall in controversy; as for example: of what is to be called right, what good, what virtue, what much, what little, what *meum* and *tuum*, what a pound, what a quart, &c. For in these things private judgements may differ and beget controversy. This common measure, some say, is right reason: with whom I should consent, if there were any such thing to be found or known *in rerum natura*. But commonly they that call for right reason to decide any controversy, do mean their own. But this is certain, seeing right reason is not existent, the reason of some man, or men, must supply the place thereof; and that man, or men, is he or they, that have the sovereign power . . .; and consequently the civil laws are to all subjects

the measures of their actions, whereby to determine, whether they be right or wrong, profitable or unprofitable, virtuous or vicious; and by them the use and definition of all names not agreed upon, and tending to controversy, shall be established. As for example, upon the occasion of some strange and deformed birth, it shall not be decided by Aristotle, or the philosophers, whether the same be a man or no, but by the laws. (II.10.8)

This was the vision at the heart of Hobbes's moral and political philosophy, and whenever he had to summarize his theory (as, for example, in the *Critique of Thomas White*—see fo. 425v), he put some version of this idea in a central position.

But the obvious problem about it is this: if politics creates the moral consensus, how is political life possible in the first place? Surely the moral disagreements of the state of nature will overwhelm any attempt to set up a civil society or commonwealth? To answer this question, Hobbes (like Grotius) shifted from talking about 'the good', which had been the traditional subject for both ancient and Renaissance moralists, to talking instead about 'rights'—a subject which the ancient and Renaissance writers had barely tackled; indeed, there is arguably no word in classical Greek or Latin for a 'right'. It was much more the traditional material of medieval scholastic moralists, and its use in a central position by both Grotius and Hobbes marked a considerable break in appearances with the humanism of their youth, though the break in substance was much less striking. But within the language of rights, Hobbes first contrived a new sceptical doubt which seemed to render even the Grotian answer to relativism untenable, and which gave rise to the most famous aspect of Hobbes's theory: the picture of men as naturally and savagely at war with one another.

Put simply, Hobbes's argument begins in the following way. There is one thing on which even in a state of nature we can all agree, and that is that other people have a right to defend themselves against attack. We can also agree that if they wish to exercise that right, they will *have* to do certain things: they cannot, for example, exercise a right of self-preservation merely by sitting around and not responding when attacked. But we will also have to recognize that in a state of nature, there will be a larger number of cases where everyone must be their own judge of how and when to defend themselves.

The consequence of this last fact is that, despite our initial agreement about the general right of self-preservation, there will in practice still be a radical instability in the state of nature. There is not much point in my saying that I agree with you in principle about your right to preserve yourself, if I disagree about whether this is the moment for you to *implement* that right. Suppose I see you walking peacefully through the primitive savannah, whistling and swinging your club: are you a danger to me? You may well think not: you have an entirely pacific disposition. But I may think you are, and the exercise of my natural right of self-preservation depends only on *my* assessment of the situation. So if I attack you, I must be justified in doing so. We have all the instability of a wholly relativist world back again, despite our agreement that people are in general justified in protecting themselves. The state of nature thus becomes a state of war, savagery, and degradation—of which, Hobbes remarked, 'present-day Americans give us an example' (*De Cive* I.13).

As I said, this is Hobbes's argument put in a simple form. Before discussing how he proposed to get from the state of nature to civil society, it is worth enlarging on the details of the argument, all of which have proved contentious for generations of Hobbes's readers.

First, what is involved in the claim that we can all agree that each of us possesses a right to defend ourselves? Hobbes expressed the claim in the following way in the *Elements of Law*:

> forasmuch as necessity of nature maketh men to will and desire *bonum sibi*, that which is good for themselves, and to avoid that which is hurtful; but most of all that terrible enemy of nature, death . . .; it is not against reason that a man doth all he can to preserve his own body and limbs,

both from death and pain. And that which is not against reason, men call RIGHT, or *jus*, or blameless liberty of using our own natural power and ability. It is therefore a *right of nature*: that every man may preserve his own life and limbs, with all the power he hath. (I.14.6)

In both *De Cive* and *Leviathan* we find almost identical formulations. On the face of it, this passage might suggest that whatever we do, we must have the right to do it, since, according to Hobbes's general theory of action, we always act in such a way as to secure what we take to be good for us; so that the right to preserve ourselves is merely a special case of this general right. A philosopher later in the seventeenth century who did in fact say just this was the Dutchman Benedict de Spinoza, who drew in many respects on Hobbes's ideas. But Hobbes did not himself ever argue such a thing; indeed, on a number of occasions he specifically said that it is possible in a state of nature to do things, and to want to do things, which we have *no* right to do. In one of the explanatory footnotes to the second edition of *De Cive*, for example, he observed that it would be impossible ever to justify drunkenness or cruelty ('that is, revenge which does not look to some future good'), since they could never be seen as conducing to our preservation (III.27). It is clear that he believed that our only natural right is the right barely to preserve ourselves, and to use whatever means we take to be necessary for that purpose.

His reasons for thinking this are not set out straightforwardly anywhere, but the limitation of our 'natural' rights to self-preservation alone is something which makes very good sense against the background of Hobbes's pessimism about human mental and emotional malleability. If we are skilled at persuasion, for example, then for our own purposes we can get other people to believe and want almost anything; the one thing we will *not* be able to persuade them is that they want their own death. At that point their fundamental nature will rebel against us. Everyone, in turn, will have to recognize this fact about other people, and thus to accept that the one common and unmalleable belief to be found among men is the belief that their own preservation is a good. Beyond that, any belief is possible. Seen in this light, Hobbes's reasons for limiting our natural rights to the special case of self-preservation were precisely the same as Grotius's: the fact that whatever else people might believe, they will have to acknowledge that all men will always, whatever the circumstances, want to preserve themselves—and that this is the *one* thing which they will always want to do. If there is to be agreement among men, it will have to be on such a basis; if we were to acknowledge other people's right to do whatever they wanted, we would have no hope of leaving the world of moral conflict.

It should be said that Hobbes took seriously one possible exception to the universality of self-preservation, the case of martyrdom for religious reasons (see *Elements of Law* II.6.14, *De Cive* XVIII.13, and *Leviathan* ch. 43, p. 625). However, as we shall see later in the section on religion, Hobbes's attitude to martyrdom altered during his life as his views about the Christian religion changed. In the earlier works he had a good reason for supposing that Christian martyrdom was a special case; in *Leviathan* he no longer had such a reason, and the discussion of martyrdom in that work is appropriately muted: Christians, he now argued, have for their faith 'the licence that Naaman had, and need not put themselves into danger for it'.

The second claim which Hobbes made, and which has proved puzzling to many readers, was the one which I summarized earlier by saying that men in a state of nature can agree that if they wish to exercise their natural right to self-preservation, they will *have* to do certain things: they cannot, for example, exercise this right merely by sitting around and not responding when attacked. Hobbes expressed this claim by talking about the *law of nature*. In the *Elements of Law* he argued as follows:

> Forasmuch as all men, carried away by the violence of their passion, and by evil custom, do those things which are commonly said to be against the law of nature; it is not the consent of passion, or consent in some error gotten by custom, that makes the law of nature. Reason is no less of the nature of man than passion, and is the same in all men,

because all men agree in the will to be directed and governed in the way to that which they desire to attain, namely their own good, which is the work of reason. There can therefore be no other law of nature than reason, nor no other precepts of NATURAL LAW, than those which declare unto us the ways of peace, where the same may be obtained, and of defence where it may not. (I.15.1)

Once again, we find virtually identical formulations in *De Cive* and *Leviathan*.

What Hobbes meant was that if you wish to preserve yourself, then it is absurd—a logical error—to suppose that you could better preserve yourself in a situation of war than one of peace. The exercise of the right of nature requires as a matter of logic that men do whatever the law of nature requires. He did not mean that men *will* always follow the precepts of the law—as he said in *De Cive* (III.26), passions and perturbations of the mind can prevent people from apprehending the truth of the precepts; 'but there is no one who is not sometimes in a quiet mind', and when in that condition they will see clearly what they must do.

The puzzle which has sometimes arisen about this argument is, what is the point of differentiating between a *right* of nature and a *law* of nature, if the general theory is that we *have* to defend ourselves and *have* to follow certain rules in order to do so? The puzzle is made particularly teasing because Hobbes actually took some care to distinguish between rights and laws: in *Leviathan* he remarked that 'RIGHT, consisteth in liberty to do, or to forbeare; Whereas LAW, determineth, and bindeth to one of them: so that Law, and Right, differ as much, as Obligation, and Liberty; which in one and the same matter are inconsistent' (ch. 14, p. 189; cf. *Elements of Law* II.10.5 and *De Cive* XIV.3). Hobbes's first readers, friendly and hostile alike, were struck by this point. As Sir Robert Filmer, one of the hostile ones, said,

If the right of nature be a liberty for a man to do anything he thinks fit to preserve his life, then in the first place nature must teach him that life is to be preserved, and so consequently forbids to do that which may destroy or take away the means of life . . .: and thus the right of nature and the law of nature will be all one: for I think Mr. Hobbes will not say the right of nature is a liberty for a man to destroy his own life . . .

But this objection, and the similar ones made by more recent writers (see Part III), miss the point of Hobbes's definition of the right of nature. In the *Elements of Law*, he said that the right was for a man to 'preserve his own life and limbs, *with all the power he hath*' (my italics), and in *Leviathan* he said (even more clearly) that the right 'is the Liberty each man hath to use his own power, *as he will himselfe*, for the preservation of his own Nature' (ch. 14, p. 189; again, my italics). The thing which Hobbes was interested in, and which made this a *right* or a *liberty* and not a duty, was that in nature we are each to do what *we* want in order to preserve ourselves. It is this openendedness, this dependence solely upon the will of the individual agent, which is important about a right, and it was this which Hobbes captured by describing our natural capacity to make our own decisions about how to protect ourselves as a right. The 'law' of nature tells us what we *ought* to decide if we are thinking rationally, but the 'right' tells us that it is we who have to decide, and that we are naturally and psychologically free to go any way we choose towards the necessary goal of our survival.

It is this fact, that is is each individual in the state of nature who decides on the route to take for his own preservation, which is captured in the third claim which I summarized above: that in the state of nature 'there will be a large number of cases where everyone must be their own judge of how and when to defend themselves'. This was the claim which split Hobbes off from Grotius (and which the Dutchman recognized as the issue between them when he read *De Cive* in 1643; Mersenne and Hobbes may even have sent him a copy). Hobbes expressed it by saying (in the words of the *Elements of Law*) that 'every man by right of nature is judge himself of the necessity of the means, and of the greatness of the danger'. This too is repeated in *De Cive* and *Leviathan*, and it was a point upon which Sir Charles Cavendish, otherwise a very friendly reader of Hobbes's work, fastened critically when he first read *De Cive* (along with the point about the relationship between the right and the law of nature). He was right to do so, since virtually the whole of what is distinctive about Hobbes's political theory follows from this simple proposition.

For if men are to be their own judges of what conduces to their preservation, all the anti-sceptical advantages of the Grotian theory are immediately lost, since by virtue of Hobbes's general philosophy, it has to be the case that there is no clear and objective truth about the external world, and that all men will make different decisions about what counts as a danger to them. But if that is so, then there will still be no agreement about what should be done, and everyone will act on the basis of their own different assessments of the situation. Conflict will arise despite the apparent solution to the relativist problem contained in the idea of a natural and universal right of self-defence. The grimmest version of sceptical relativism seems after all to be the only possible ethical vision; and for ethics taken independently of politics, this is indeed Hobbes's conclusion.

Politics

However, Hobbes was able to provide a solution to his own version of ethical relativism, a solution which gave him in the end a genuine political theory. He tried various ways of expressing it; in each of the three major political works there is a slightly different formulation, but the general idea is essentially the same. It was that men in a state of nature will come to see, in their reflective moments, that the law of nature obliges them to renounce their right of private judgement over what is to count as dangerous in dubious cases, and to accept for themselves the judgement of a common authority. In the *Elements of Law* Hobbes tried to express this by talking about a renunciation of the right of nature *itself*; what he meant was the full right of nature, as defined in that work—that is, the right to use 'all the power' we have to defend ourselves—but it was a confusing way of putting the idea, since (as he conceded) a man cannot renounce the basic right to defend himself *in extremis*. In *Leviathan* he produced the most satisfactory formula: a common authority is created when everyone in a state of nature agrees 'to submit their Wills, every one to his Will, and their Judgements, to his Judgement (ch. 17, p. 227). Even in the *Elements of Law*, however, he had put the idea simply enough when he said that the 'sum' of the laws of nature 'consisteth in forbidding us to be our own judges, and our own carvers' (I.17.10).

By the terms of Hobbes's account of the state of nature, conflict arises because people judge differently about what is a danger to them, and the fact that they judge differently is enough to show that there is an inherent dubiousness about the cases in questions—a view similar to the attitude expressed in a remark he made in another context in the *Elements of Law*, that 'the infallible sign of teaching exactly, and without error, is this: that no man hath ever taught the contrary; not that few, how few soever' (I.13.3). There is no *fact of the matter* in these doubtful cases, and people therefore have no reason to prefer their own judgement to that of another person. Since they do have a most powerful reason for wanting their judgement aligned with other people's, it is a simple conclusion to draw that they should all find some single source of opinion whose view about the danger to each of them in doubtful or contentious cases they will accept. Its power will then protect its citizens, for it will be able to co-ordinate their judgements round the same dangers, and elicit common action against both criminals and other nations who pose a possible threat to the new 'commonwealth' which the citizens have thus brought into being. This common judge is by definition the *sovereign* over the commonwealth, though it need not be a single person: a single will, even it if is the decision of an assembly of some kind, is all that is necessary. Hobbes gave in all three of his political works some rather low-level reasons for preferring monarchy to other forms of government, but his theory applies indiscriminately to all types of government, including republics. Hobbes's theory is neatly summed up in a remark he made in Chapter 37 of *Leviathan* where he described the sovereign as 'Gods Lieutenant; to whom in all doubtfull cases, we have submitted our private judgements' (p. 477).

It remains true, however, that where it is absolutely clear to an individual citizen that his life is in danger—where no one could dispute it—then of course he must defend it himself, whatever the sovereign might say: 'A man cannot lay down the right of resisting them, that assault him by force, to take away his life; because he cannot be understood to ayme thereby, at any Good to himself' (*Leviathan* ch. 14, p. 192). This applies even if it is the sovereign himself, or his agents, who are assaulting him:

> for man by nature chooseth the lesser evill, which is danger of death in resisting; rather than the greater, which is certain and present death in not resisting. And this is granted to be true by all men, in that they lead Criminals to Execution, and Prison, with armed men, notwithstanding that such Criminals have consented to the Law, by which they are condemned. (Ibid., p. 199)

Hobbes found himself in something of a tactical quandary in his early formulations of this theory. In both the *Elements of Law* (II.1.2–3) and *De Cive* (VI.1) he claimed that the common submission of a disunited 'multitude' to a sovereign made the multitude one 'person', though it was a person only as long as it had a sovereign. He recorded in one of the footnotes to the second edition of *De Cive* (1647) that this had puzzled many readers, though he continued in that note to insist on it; but it was a dangerous position to take up, for it allowed the multitude a unity, albeit through the existence of a common sovereign, which might in principle be used *against* its sovereign. Hobbes wished to refute the idea repeatedly put forward in the English Civil War, that 'the People' had the collective right to limit their sovereign, but this early formulation in fact lent some credence to it. But in *Leviathan* he worked out an elaborate theory according to which all the members of a multitude are individually 'impersonated' or 'represented' by their sovereign, and the only unity is that possessed by the sovereign's will. 'For it is the *Unity* of the Representer, not the *Unity* of the Represented, that maketh the Person *One*. And it is the Representer that beareth the Person, and but one Person: And *Unity*, cannot otherwise be understood in Multitude' (ch. 16, p. 220; contrast particularly *De Cive* VI.1 note).

A question sometimes raised about Hobbes's theory of the origin of sovereignty is that it seems to rule out the possibility of men ever fighting for their sovereign, since it must always be better to avoid participating in a war than to run the risk of dying on the battlefield or being killed when trying to arrest a criminal. Yet Hobbes says (*Leviathan* ch. 21, p. 270) that 'when the Defence of the Common-wealth, requireth at once the help of all that are able to bear Arms, every one is obliged'. But if we think of the sovereign as making decisions for us in doubtful cases about what is a threat, then we can see that bearing arms for our country is rational: for it has just the same *rationale* as fighting against a presumed enemy in the state of nature. The only difference is that the sovereign is now doing the presuming, rather than us ourselves. This issue is, I think, one of the central issues with which Hobbes was originally concerned, for it was precisely the topic at issue during the Ship Money crisis of 1636 onwards: is it purely up to the sovereign to determine if, say, the Dutch are a threat to the English, or can individual Englishmen have an opinion on the matter? Hobbes's answer to this is clearly in line with that of the Royalist judges in the Ship Money case: only the King has the right to pronounce on the question of where England's vital interests lie, and his subjects must pay or fight as he decrees.

A similar problem, but one much harder to deal with, which is frequently raised about Hobbes's account of the generation of a commonwealth, is that he talks about it in terms of a *promise* or *contract* made by the inhabitants of the state of nature to co-ordinate their activities round a particular sovereign. But why should any of them keep this promise if it turns out to be to their advantage later to break it? This is made particularly problematical by Hobbes's general claim that in a state of nature no one could ever have a reason to keep their promises, 'because the bonds of words are too weak to bridle mens ambition, avarice, anger, and other Passions, without the fear of some coercive power' (*Leviathan* ch. 14, p. 196).

Hobbes's discussion of promising, at least in *Leviathan* (where it is most completely thought out), goes as follows. His fundamental point is that if two (or more) people promise each other to do something (in the case of the fundamental social contract, to respect the decisions of the same sovereign), then *if* one person keeps his word, the others have no good reason not to keep theirs. They have no good reason, because the only good reasons are those of self-preservation; and someone who has done what he said he would do is not a danger to other people. On these grounds, Hobbes argues in Chapter 15 of *Leviathan* (p. 203) that only a 'Foole' would say 'there is no such thing as Justice'—justice consisting precisely in keeping one's word if others have done likewise. The question then is simply, what can motivate someone in the state of nature into being the *first* person to keep his word? Hobbes himself seems to say that there can be *no* rational motive to do so: in a state of nature, 'he that performest first, has no assurance the other will performe after . . . And therefore he which performeth first, does but betray himselfe his enemy' (ch. 14. p. 196). So the puzzle remains: how is the social contract possible?

There is, I think, no easy answer to this question to be extracted from the Hobbesian texts; the fact that Hobbes tried several slightly different ways of putting his idea about the construction of the commonwealth suggests that he found difficulties here too. What one might say is that Hobbes's remarks about the impossibility of making covenants or keeping promises in a state of nature are part of a very general account of promise-keeping. Clearly, for most promises it will indeed be true that one is delivering oneself into the hands of an enemy if one performs one's own side of a bargain before he does: but it is not too clear that this is true of the promise to regard the sovereign's judgement as one's own. This promise, it must be stressed, is made not to the sovereign but to the other prospective citizens, and one will presumably be no worse off in one's dealings with *them* after keeping one's word, even if they do not keep theirs, than one would have been in the state of nature anyway. All that has changed is that judgements about the threat posed by other men in doubtful cases are now made for me by another person; but precisely because they are doubtful cases, I have no reason to suppose that the judgements will be any worse than my own were, and therefore no reason to suppose that I will be worse off following my sovereign even if the others do not. So I may as well keep my word, and see what the others do.

But equally, it should be said, I will be no better off following him unless the others do likewise: I will effectively remain in the same state as I was before, surrounded by men with disparate judgements about when to exercise the right of self-preservation. If this is a situation which is likely to persist, then there is simply no point in transferring my right of private judgement to the sovereign, and I may as well go back to looking after myself in all instances. This is a point which Hobbes particularly stressed in the 'Review and Conclusion' he tacked on to the end of *Leviathan*, for it was what justified, in his opinion, the transference of allegiance by Englishmen from the Crown to the new republic. They were no longer 'protected' by the Crown, and there is 'a mutuall Relation between Protection and Obedience' (p. 728)—a slogan frequently used in the pamphlet literature in England during 1649–51 in relation to submission to the new regime.

This account of the foundational contract puts the matter in terms which Hobbes himself did not use, but it is arguably loyal to the general character of his idea. It enables us to accept that such a contract is possible, and we can now turn to the specifically political aspects of Hobbes's theory, and in particular to his discussion of the rights of sovereigns over their citizens.

The common impression of Hobbes is of a theorist of absolute state power, an impression fostered by the very title of *Leviathan* and by the description of the sovereign as 'that great LEVIATHAN, or rather (to speake more reverently) . . . that *Mortall God*' (p. 227). But there are some important qualifications to be introduced, which derive from Hobbes's conception of the fundamental character of sovereign power. As we have seen, the sovereign *represents* the citizens, in the sense that his judgement about dangers is (by and large) to count as their judgement. The considerations which govern the sovereign's actions are therefore the same as those which govern anyone's actions in the state of nature, namely, how best to secure a situation in which he will be at least risk from attack. His citizens' safety will, Hobbes believed, be caught up in his own; and he tended to gloss over the complexity of the actual relationship between a sovereign's preservation and that of his citizens. In *Leviathan*, at least, he frequently talks about the sovereign acting in some sense on behalf of his citizens, and seems to regard it as rational for a sovereign to do whatever he sincerely believes conduces to his own preservation and that of the people he represents. For the sovereign to do anything else, he repeatedly says (for example ch. 24, p. 297), would be 'a breach of trust, and of the Law of Nature'—though, as we shall see, he did not conclude from the fact that a sovereign might have no right to do something, that a subject might have the right to resist him.

What this meant was that many things which a conventional theory of absolute state power would allow are ruled out on Hobbes's account of the sovereign's rights. Perhaps the most striking example of this is the question of *private property*. It follows from Hobbes's account of the fundamental right of nature that everyone is entitled to the material objects necessary for their survival: food, water, housing, and so on. There is therefore a minimal level of private property, at least of a kind, in the state of nature; Hobbes further argued that men in a state of nature would not be entitled to amass more than was necessary for their own preservation, if by doing so they deprived others of the necessities of life:

> It is supposed to be incumbent upon everyone to acquire the necessities of life, not only by *right* but also by *natural necessity*. So if any one wishes to compete for more than this, he will be guilty of starting a war, since there was no

need for him to fight for anything; he will therefore be breaking *the fundamental law of nature*. (*De Cive* III.9; see also *Leviathan* ch. 15, p. 209)

As long as men teeter economically on the edge of survival, therefore, it is morally wrong (according to Hobbes) for some people to amass more than they need.

This general principle holds good in a commonwealth too. In *Leviathan* Hobbes argues that the particular distribution of land and resources in a society must be thought of as originally the decision of the sovereign. This was a frequently expressed view at the time, at least in the form of the claim that a particular property distribution is the consequence of a particular system of civil law. Grotius, for example, believed that to be the case. But Hobbes says that

> seeing the Soveraign, that is to say, the Common-wealth (whose Person he representeth,) is understood to do nothing but in order to the common Peace and Security, this Distribution of lands, is to be understood as done in order to the same: And consequently, whatsoever Distribution another shall make in prejudice thereof, is contrary to the will of every subject, that committed his Peace, and safety to his discretion, and conscience; and therefore by the will of every one of them, is to be reputed voyd ... (ch. 24, p. 297) [the reading 'another' will not be found in any printed text, but is based on the manuscript of *Leviathan*]

So if the distribution of property works in such a way that people are physically endangered by it, and members of the commonwealth do not have access to the material necessities of life, then the sovereign is required to intervene and redistribute it; he must always ensure that everyone has at least the minimum necessary for survival. In Chapter 30 of *Leviathan*, Hobbes argues that the commonwealth must be responsible for the provision of maintenance for the destitute: 'they ought not to be left to the Charity of private persons; but to be provided for, (as far-forth as the necessities of Nature require,) by the Lawes of the Common-wealth' (p. 387). A corollary of this, however, was that the sovereign must have the right to tax people to the level he thinks fit in order to protect the commonwealth: no 'right of private property' can be pleaded against his actions, as had been argued during the Ship Money controversy.

Furthermore, it seems that Hobbes's sovereign could not have the right to implement any policy (such as, say, a regime of strict egalitarianism) just because he thought it was a good idea. The only right of ours which the sovereign possesses, or which he exercises on our behalf, is the right to consider what means are necessary to our survival, and it would not therefore be on the basis of *our* rights that he would introduce any programme which went beyond the considerations of physical survival. Those considerations could take a sovereign a long way, it should be conceded: general economic prosperity, for example, might reasonably be thought to damp down civil conflict, so whatever made a nation prosperous would come to seem justified under the terms of Hobbes's theory. Hobbes indeed borrowed a great deal from contemporary accounts of how to increase a nation's prosperity—the literature of the movement subsequently known as 'mercantilism'. But at some point a sovereign might try to introduce policies which could not be justified in these terms, and at that point it would be possible to say that he had exceeded his rights. This would be particularly true if the policies were of a kind to arouse antagonism on the part of some section of the commonwealth, for the sovereign would then be endangering his own survival for no *necessary* reason. Accordingly, Hobbes, for example (*Leviathan* ch. 30, p. 386), while fully supporting a sovereign's right to level taxes without the consent of the taxed, argued against the legitimacy of egalitarian taxation, or income tax, preferring instead taxation on articles of consumption.

Hobbes's sovereign is thus, from the point of view of modern political assumptions, an ambiguous figure: possessed of great and apparently illiberal powers, there are nevertheless some things he cannot (or, more properly, *should* not) do which a modern state would regard as unquestionably legitimate. The vital point is that Hobbes's theory embodies the paradoxes of early or classical *liberalism* (and in this respect is not very different from, for example, John Locke's ideas). The primary responsibility of both citizens and sovereigns is to ensure the physical survival of themselves and their fellow citizens. Once this minimal requirement has been met, policies should not be enforced upon the community—though that requirement in fact implies a considerable degree of state power. Nineteenth- or twentieth-century exponents of *laissez-faire* in a sense took for granted the achievement of physical survival; for seventeenth-century liberals, both public order and a minimum level of subsistence were hard-won prizes. Nor should it be forgotten that it was only in Hobbes's lifetime that Western Europeans became more or less the first people in the history of our planet who could reasonably expect not to face devastating famine at some point in their lives.

A similar paradox is to be found in the last area of the sovereign's power which I want to consider, his rights over public debate and doctrine. More than anything else in Hobbes's theory, it has been the sovereign's total right to legislate on intellectual matters which has alarmed his readers, from the seventeenth century to our own time. Hobbes was absolutely clear that the sovereign had this right:

> it is annexed to the Soveraignty, to be Judge of what Opinions and Doctrines are averse, and what conducing to Peace; and consequently, on what occasions, how farre, and what, men are to be trusted withall, in speaking to Multitudes of people; and who shall examine the Doctrines of all bookes before they be published. For the Actions of men proceed from their Opinions; and in the well governing of Opinions, consisteth the well government of mens Actions, in order to their Peace, and Concord. And though in matter of Doctrine, nothing ought to be regarded but the Truth; yet this is not repugnant to regulating of the same by Peace . . . (*Leviathan* ch. 18, p. 233).

As this passage illustrates, the rationale for Hobbes's position was drawn straightforwardly from his fundamental presuppositions—that the alignment of opinion and judgement upon which the commonwealth rests cannot take place unless the sovereign is to be fully the judge of what men should be taught or might hear (for what they hear might persuade them). This seems on the face of it to be diametrically opposed to the most basic liberal assumptions.

However, once again we have to remember that we are dealing with the seventeenth century—and that what alarmed some of his readers then may have been very different from what would alarm us today. As I shall show in the next section, Hobbes's primary object in arguing like this was to elevate the power of the sovereign over the *churches*—bands of fanatics (in his eyes) who wished to enforce absurd opinions upon their fellow citizens, and whose activities were primarily responsible for the civil wars of Europe. They could only be controlled if the sovereign was empowered to determine public doctrine and silence disputes. But his was essentially a *negative* role: to align opinions, not to work hard in order to secure the acceptance of any *particular* point of view. The modern liberal fear of totalitarianism (especially after the experiences of the twentieth century) is primarily that the State will have its own ideological axe to grind, that it will force racist doctrines or particular economic theories upon its citizens. But for Hobbes and his contemporaries, the State was almost definable as the body in a society which has no ideological axe of its own. Though surrounded by dogmatists, there was no reason why the State itself should be wedded to any dogma other than the need to secure the survival of its citizens.

Apart from the churches, there was one other group of people whose views Hobbes wished to see the sovereign regulate; ironically, this was the group to which he himself had belonged in his youth, the *humanists*. *Leviathan* in particular is full of denunciations of the evil effects of studying the Greek and Roman classics, which, he said, had led their readers into mistaken ideas about *liberty*. Athens and Rome were republics, and to bolster their sovereignty they had appropriately taught their citizens the superiority of republican government; but reading the ancient classics out of this context had misled people into praising republican liberty as a universal value, and into seeking to reconstruct their own societies on republican lines—so that 'I think I may truly say, there was never any thing so deerly bought, as these Western parts have bought the learning, of the Greek and Latine tongues'. Hobbes conceded that 'the libertie, whereof there is so frequent, and honourable mention, in the Histories, and Philosophy of the Antient Greeks, and Romans' (*Leviathan* ch. 21, p. 266), did have a value; but only when understood as the liberty of the commonwealth from external pressure, rather than the liberty of the subject. This concession in fact reveals his disinclination fully to slough off his early humanism, for it was a view shared by many humanists (including, arguably, Machiavelli)—though those humanists had also argued that the citizens of a free commonwealth would *ipso facto* be freer themselves, and it was this claim which Hobbes repudiated. Hobbes summed up his view in a memorable passage about the Italian city of Lucca, which he must have visited, and which still displays the inscriptions he noticed:

> There is written on the Turrets of the city of *Luca* in great characters at this day, the word LIBERTAS; yet no man can thence inferre, that a particular man has more Libertie, or Immunitie from the service of the Commonwealth there, than in *Constantinople*. Whether a Commonwealth be Monarchicall, or Popular, the Freedome is still the same (p. 266)

Though in the regulation of public doctrine, trade, and private property, there might (according to Hobbes) be limitations on a sovereign's right to pursue his own programme beyond what the laws of nature prescribe, these limitations have to be understood as moral duties upon the sovereign, rather than as rights which his subjects can enforce against him. The distinction was an important one for Hobbes, for it was a key part of his theory that though one might say that a sovereign had broken the laws of nature in some way, one could not thereby claim the right immediately to resist him. Again, we have to draw a precise parallel with the ethical features of the state of nature. In that state, the fact that another person had broken the laws of nature (had, for example, got drunk) would not have given us some extra right to attack him: it would have been foolish and self-destructive conduct on his part, but irrelevant to the question of our own rights and duties. The same is true of the citizens' relations with their sovereign: until he actually starts to attack them, or until all government breaks down, what he does is irrelevant to the question of whether they ought to obey him. As a matter of fact, persistent incompetence by a sovereign is likely to antagonize people so much that they will eventually be led to rebel—though such a rebellion would be morally unjustified unless the actual survival of the rebels was at stake.

The narrowness of the right which the citizen possesses against the sovereign—a narrowness which seems (and indeed is) so markedly against fundamental liberal assumptions—is thus a function of the general narrowness of the rights which people possess under any circumstances; and that in turn, as we have seen, is a function of the impossibility of finding an agreed, coherent, and compelling moral theory of any elaborateness or complexity. In this area more than any other, perhaps, we have to face the fact that moral relativism—which is something to which many modern liberals would instinctively subscribe—may well issue in illiberal politics, and was almost universally taken by its first major exponents actually to do so. It may well be that Locke, who is the most obvious example of someone at the time who managed to avoid these political conclusions, was only able to avoid them because he had a more extensive and dogmatic ethical theory, which most of his modern readers are inclined to ignore; but whether liberalism of his kind can survive without such a theory remains an open question.

Religion

Only the politically radical in the seventeenth century read Hobbes as a fearsome theorist of state power; it was also quite possible to see his work instead as being corrosive of existing regimes—many conservatives, in fact, objected to it on just these grounds. But what made Hobbes almost uniformly alarming to his contemporaries, as I have already remarked in Part I, were his views on *religion*; and there is little doubt that it is his reputation for atheism, whether covert or overt, which has fuelled most discussion about his work since then. In this section I want to assess the real character of Hobbes's religious beliefs, and explain why they seem to have changed in the course of his life. We must distinguish, however, between his views on religion *in general*—the existence and character of a God—and his views on the *Christian* religion. While the former changed very little during his life, the latter changed markedly, and it seems to have been this change which most alienated his readers.

As we saw in the first section of Part II, the issue of the existence and character of a God was central to the debate about Descartes in which Hobbes was immersed in the late 1630s, and his writing from 1640 to 1643 make his own theological position perfectly clear. To understand it, we have first to remember that Hobbes argued in his metaphysics that the material upon which (so to speak) the mind works is made up of 'fantasies' or mental images, caused by inscrutable external forces. We can deduce from the existence of these fantasies something of the general character of the world—in particular, that it is composed of material objects interacting causally with one another—but we can know with certainty nothing else. Hobbes's fundamental claim about God was that it is absolutely impossible to form such a mental image of him. As he said in his Objections to Descartes's *Meditations* of 1641,

> to say that God is *independent* [i.e. uncaused] is simply to say that God belongs to the class of things such that I cannot image their origin. Similarly, to say that God is *infinite* is the same as saying that he belongs to the class of things such that we do not conceive of them as having bounds. It follows that any idea of God is ruled out. For what sort of idea is it which has no origin and no limits?

The same could be said, he observed in the *Elements of Law*, about all the conventional qualities attributed to God: 'all his attributes signify our inability and defect of power to conceive any thing concerning his nature' (I.10.2).

Since philosophy, according to Hobbes, can only concern itself with mental images and their implications, there is no place for God in philosophy—with one exception. Hobbes's metaphysics presupposed a sequence of causal relations, with each change in the world being brought about by some earlier moving body. At some inconceivably remote point in time—an 'infinity' ago—that sequence must have begun, and the 'first cause' could be described philosophically as 'God'. Hobbes, it should be said, believed that 'infinity' meant simply a quantity which human beings as a matter of fact could not count or measure. 'When someone says something is 'uncountable' we believe we understand that term. We do not, on hearing it, go mad or play the metaphysician, as we do on hearing the word 'infinite', yet both mean the same thing' (*Critique of Thomas White* fo. 330). So he accepted the possibility of a really existing first cause some uncountable number of years ago, though what it might have been like he could not say—modern astrophysicists' 'Big Bang' might have played the same role as 'God' for him. The crucial point is that all the conventional attributes of God such as benevolence and omnipotence were excluded from the *philosophical* concept of God.

But an impersonal, philosophical God of this kind still had an important role to play in Hobbes's theory. First, Hobbes argued in all his major works that there is a 'natural religion'. Whatever made the universe and therefore ourselves must be incomparably more powerful than anything else we can imagine, and it is a psychological truth that power of this kind necessarily elicits worship (*De Cive* XV.9; this whole chapter is the main discussion by Hobbes of natural religion). As part of our worship, we can use any language which tends to express our feelings; but this language (the language of any conventional religion) 'pertains not to the explanation of philosophical truth, but to proclaiming the states of mind that govern our wish to praise, magnify and honour God' (*Critique of Thomas White* fo. 396). All religions, Hobbes claimed, are simply ways of worshipping this inscrutable creator, and their doctrines and practices are whatever are deemed culturally appropriate as acts of worship. The institution responsible for deeming them was of course the commonwealth: 'the commonwealth [*civitas*] (that is, those who possess the power of the whole commonwealth) by right decides which *names* or *appellations* give honour to God and which do not; that is, which doctrines about the nature and works of God should be publically held and professed' (*De Cive* XV.16). But though the specific religion available in a society was a civil matter, and though Hobbes clearly aligned himself with those theorists such as Machiavelli who argued for a 'civil religion'—a tradition culminating in Rousseau—he was equally clear that it is rational to have a religion. Atheism, as he made clear in *De Cive* XIV.19, is a 'sin'; but it is a sin of 'imprudence or ignorance' only, by which he meant that it is like the denial of any other philosophically compelling argument.

Furthermore, this inscrutable creator could be thought of as the progenitor of the laws of nature. Thus Hobbes remarked in the *Elements of Law*, 'forasmuch as law (to speak properly) is a command, and these dictates, as they proceed from nature, are not commands; they are not therefore called laws in respect of nature, but in respect of the author of nature, God Almighty' (I.17.12). Hobbes was always slightly troubled by the fact that the principles which men ought rationally to follow in order to secure their preservation were termed 'laws', since 'law' normally implies the existence of a law*giver*; the modern use of the terms 'scientific law' or 'law of nature', as in the 'law of gravity', which carries of course no religious implications, lay some way in the future in Hobbes's lifetime. But he never advanced the view (which some modern scholars have attributed to him) that the *reason* for doing what the laws prescribe is that they are the commands of God: our reason for following them is that they are general principles which tell us how to preserve ourselves effectively. We do not have to know that there is a God in order to know that we must follow the laws of nature, because we obviously do not *need* to know that there is a first cause in order to believe any other true propositions about the world, and no other idea of God is admissible into philosophy. Hobbes registered this fact when, in addition to describing atheism as a sin of ignorance, he denied that it was a sin of 'injustice', or 'against the law of nature'. It should be said that he accepted this would not be true if God happened to be a civil sovereign, as had been the case for the Jews; but that was obviously a special case.

Hobbes's idea of a natural religion can fairly be described as 'deist', and his blend of deism and civil religion was to prove prophetic of much Enlightenment thinking. Like the Enlightenment writers, he took ancient religions to be paradigmatic, remarking in the *Elements of Law* that 'among the Grecians, Romans, or other Gentiles . . . their several civil laws were the rules whereby not only righteousness and virtue, but also religion and the external worship of God, was ordered and approved; that being esteemed the true worship of God, which was κατὰ τὰ νόμινα [*kata ta nomina*] (*i.e.*), according to the laws civil' (II.6.2). Religion in antiquity was thus like morality, the preserve of the State, with only the minimal 'natural religion' of God the creator as a common core to the different religions.

Such a narrow definition of natural or philosophical religion was contentious in Hobbes's own time, but it was by no means unusual or heretical: many contemporary theologians would have concurred that philosophical reasoning could tell men little about God. The idea that reason could deliver a full theology was primarily held by Aristotelians, committed by their general philosophy to the claim that rational common sense could tell men all truths about the world (a claim we have already seen being made in the context of discussions about sense-perception). By 1640 plenty of orthodox theologians, both Catholic and Protestant, were critical of Aristotle and sympathetic to the general sceptical case against him; but they reconciled this scepticism with their theology by insisting that belief in a Christian God, with all the properties conventionally attributed to him, must rest exclusively on *faith*.

But this tendency, which the nineteenth century dubbed 'fideism', took various forms, and to understand Hobbes's theology we need to see the difference between him and the fideists. Broadly speaking, there were three different fideistic ideas among orthodox theologians. The first and most implausible (though probably the commonest, at least among an older generation) was simply that to be a Christian was to believe in a Christian God, in the Incarnation and Redemption, etc., and that no reason could be given for this faith, though it could be explained within its own terms (by talking about God's good will in granting the believer his beliefs). This is rather like the approach to ethics which holds that everyone simply makes their own ethical commitment, and no reasons can be given for making one kind of commitment rather than another; like that approach, it most plausibly ends in relativism and pluralism. But religious pluralism was the last thing most orthodox theologians wanted, and two other kinds of fideism were advanced to meet this objection.

One was associated particularly with an early seventeenth-century follower of Montaigne, the Frenchman Pierre Charron. In many respects Charron was a pure sceptic, whose criticisms of Aristotelian philosophy were among the most cogent produced by the Renaissance sceptics. But he coupled this scepticism with an argument for a belief in Christianity (and, specifically, Catholic Christianity) which utilized one of the basic sceptical ideas. As we saw in Part I, the scepticism of men like Montaigne or Lipsius issued in a recommendation to men to do whatever was necessary to preserve themselves, from physical attack or emotional turmoil; Charron simply argued that religious belief is psychologically very sustaining and cheering. One will feel more content, and less troubled by the world, if one is religious; and in a Catholic country, one will be physically as well as mentally safer adopting Catholicism. The *truth* of the belief was irrelevant, since truths of this sort could not be determined; so Charron's argument presupposed that the content of religion was a matter of faith rather than reason. But there could be a good reason for having faith.

Charron's approach remained popular with a number of Christians, particularly in his native country—perhaps the most famous is Blaise Pascal who, later in the seventeenth century, elaborated a similar argument for Christianity. But, like the earlier form of fideism, it was basically relativist: in different countries and at different times, Charron's argument implies, man will rightly choose different religions. His argument could justify the existing distribution of religious beliefs and practices, but it could not help anyone faced by a stark choice between evenly balanced doctrines. Moreover, it was itself vulnerable to scepticism: Paolo Sarpi, leader of Venice during the Interdict Crisis (with whose circle of followers Hobbes was familiar, as we saw in Part I), argued in a series of unpublished reflections that political and psychological considerations of this kind would not necessarily lead to people adopting a religion of *any* kind; the states of the ancient world, he argued, had managed perfectly well by instilling a wholly secular sense of honour and patriotism into their citizens. Sarpi has some claim to be the first systematic thinker who denied any social efficacy for religion: even Hobbes was unwilling to go so far, though it is quite possible that he was influenced to some extent by his ideas.

The last variety of fideism was intended to avoid the problems which the other two approaches raised. This version is associated mainly with England, and a group of English theologians in the 1630s, among whom Hobbes had many friends. It was expressed particularly well in a classic of Anglican theology, William Chillingworth's *The Religion of Protestants* (1638). (Chillingworth was a close friend of Hobbes before the Civil War; he died in a Parliamentary prison in 1644). Chillingworth argued that we have as good reason to believe many of the stories about Christ as we do to believe in any historical events which we have not ourselves witnessed. It is a mistake to think that we need some special and mysterious kind of faith to be religious; it is true that we cannot demonstrate logically and philosophically the existence of a God or the truth of the Christian revelation, but nor can we demonstrate the former existence of Henry VIII. We do, however, have reasons of a universal, cross-cultural kind for taking some things on trust.

Chillingworth and his friends aligned themselves on this issue very much with Grotius, who devoted the last twenty years of his life before his death in 1645 to arguing that

Christianity was not a mysterious matter and that it could be defended against critics from other religions. A belief in 'at least one God' who made the world and cares for it was, Grotius said, as universal a human phenomenon as the principle of self-preservation, and therefore as unquestionable; this was the foundation of Grotius's 'natural religion', which was very close in spirit to Hobbes's. But this natural or primitive religion should be supplemented by Christianity, which had an advantage over all competing religions in that it was both more soundly based on a historical record, and required—or should require—fewer contentious beliefs on the part of its adherents. Grotius compared it in this respect particularly with the complicated ritual prescriptions of Judaism, and the military dogmas of Islam. The 'Grotian Religion' (as it was termed by one of his opponents) became popular in the most advanced Anglican circles on the eve of the Civil War, and the goal of a minimalist Christianity was set alongside the goal of a minimalist ethics as a solution to relativism.

As one might have expected, it is this English strain of fideism which is prominent in Hobbes's early works. In the *Elements of Law* he distinguishes clearly between *knowledge* and *opinion*, that is, between beliefs which are certain and those which are not; he describes faith as an opinion 'admitted out of trust to other men' (I.6.7). The critical issue, for Hobbes as for everyone else, was the status of belief in the validity of the Christian religion, particularly as set out in the Scriptures; and he explained faith in the truth of Scripture in terms of our confidence in the accurate transmission of the record:

> Seeing then the acknowledgement of the Scriptures to be the word of God, is not evidence [i.e. evident to natural reason], but faith; and faith . . . consisteth in the trust we have in other men: it appeareth plainly that the men so trusted, are the holy men of God's church succeeding one another from the time of those that saw the wondrous works of God Almighty in the flesh . . . (I.11.9)

A number of obvious problems immediately pose themselves about this position, all of which Hobbes tried to answer. The first is, does his general metaphysics not rule out at least some of the traditional dogmas of Christianity? How can a denial of the possibility of incorporeal objects, for example, square with the frequent references in the Bible to 'spirits'? Hobbes argued here that, on the one hand, talk of God as a 'spirit' was merely a result of our incapacity to think of him in material terms, and on the other that 'though the Scripture acknowledge spirits, yet doth it nowhere say, they are incorporeal' (I.11.5): a materialist explanation of all the events in the Bible was possible, and such an explanation would not, Hobbes claimed, deny the fundamentals of Christianity.

The second problem is, then, what are the fundamentals of Christianity? What are we believing if we take the Scriptures to be authoritative? Hobbes's answer here remained the same throughout his life: under the terms of our Christian faith, we are required to believe only 'that Jesus is the Messiah, that is, the Christ (II.6.6). Hobbes understood by this that Jesus is the Saviour—that the former existence of Christ on earth will cause those who believe in his existence to have eternal life. In his early work he did not explain how eternal life might be compatible with a materialist metaphysics, but in *Leviathan* (as we shall see presently) he went to some trouble to show that the two things were compatible. Hobbes's view of the fundamentals of Christianity broadly resembled Grotius's: once again, he was following the Dutchman along the path towards minimalism.

Thirdly, but in some ways the crucial problem, who is to be authoritative in the interpretation of Scripture? We can have a general confidence that the scriptural record is historically accurate, but there are difficulties in understanding such a complex document, and we need a source of confidence in one reading rather than another. This source could be our own private judgement, but Hobbes was always very opposed to this—naturally enough, since it restored exactly the randomness of opinion which plagued the state of nature. In both the *Elements of Law* and *De Cive*, however, the authoritative interpretation of the Scriptures is not left (as one might have expected) to the *sovereign*, but to the *Church*:

Seeing our faith, that the Scriptures are the word of God, began from the confidence and trust we repose in the church; there can be no doubt but that their interpretation of the same Scriptures, when any doubt or controversy shall arise, by which this fundamental point, that Jesus is come in the flesh, is not called into question, is safer for any man to trust to, than his own, whether reasoning, or spirit; that is to say his own opinion. (I.11.10)

The last problem is the relationship between the Church and the State. Here, Hobbes argued two things in his earlier works. First, in matters of natural reason or philosophy, the sovereign must have absolute power to determine the meanings of words and the content of public belief (for the reasons set out in the previous section). Secondly, where the Christian faith is concerned, though the sovereign's pronouncements are also to be authoritative for his citizens, a Christian sovereign is himself *obliged* to interpret the Scriptures 'through properly ordained Clergymen' (*De Cive* XVII.28). This is because Christ himself promised an 'infallibility' in the interpretation of those doctrines which are necessary to salvation to 'his *Apostles* until the day of judgement, that is to the *Apostles* and the *Priests* following the Apostles and consecrated by the laying-on of hands' (ibid).

Hobbes thus compromised the unity of his theory in this one respect, for he allowed (albeit in a kind of advisory position) a crucial role to the Church in the formation of public doctrine. With the one difficult and contentious exception of his materialism, in fact, Hobbes's religious ideas as set before his public by 1642 were extremely close to orthodox Anglicanism. Like the English Grotians, he wanted a minimalist Christianity; like Chillingworth he treated faith as a matter of confidence in a historical record; like all Anglicans he combined a belief in the supremacy of the sovereign in doctrinal matters with a commitment to the special role of the apostolic church in prescribing what dogmas the sovereign should enforce upon his citizens. It is not surprising, therefore, that many of his friends in the 1630s should have been devout clergymen, and that there was little hostility from them towards either the *Elements of Law* or *De Cive*.

But, as we saw in Part I, all this changed with the appearance of *Leviathan*, when the serious possibility was raised of regarding Hobbes as an atheist—the charge which was to plague his later years. As we also saw in Part I, the reason for the shift probably lay partly in Hobbes's enthusiasm for the anti-Presbyterian struggle, in which he saw Independency as having the best chance of winning; but another part of the reason lay, I think, in Hobbes's increasing awareness of the real implications of his general philosophical position.

The change came about through Hobbes's abandonment of his old view about the interpretation of Scripture; yet this apparently technical move was sufficient to make a dramatic difference in his religious theory. The fundamental distinction between philosophy and faith went through unaltered into *Leviathan*, as did the philosophical understanding of God as a first cause. But at great length and in minute detail, Hobbes now sought to show that the only interpreter of Scripture could be the civil sovereign, and that there was nothing special about a *church* at all. The apostolic succession from Christ through the sequential laying-on of hands, upon which he had placed so much stress in *De Cive*, was now dismissed as unimportant (ch. 42, pp. 571–5), on the basis of elaborate scholarship (much of which, it should be said, he owed to some of Grotius's recently published theological works—though characteristically he failed to acknowledge this fact). What form a church took, therefore, and what doctrines its clergy taught, were now to be determined solely and entirely by the *fiat* of the sovereign; there was no authoritative body beside him, obliging him to promulgate a particular interpretation of Scripture. The general rights of the sovereign over the meanings of words now extended to include all the meanings of all God's word also.

In many ways, of course, this position made much better sense than his earlier one, for it now aligned religious beliefs with other contentious beliefs in the domain controlled by the sovereign. But it had two particular consequences, both of which were disturbing to his old friends. The first concerned the question of ecclesiastical organization, and the second the question of theological dogma.

As regards the first, Hobbes now drew the natural conclusion that if there was nothing special about an apostolically ordained church, then there was no reason why a sovereign should in general be interested in maintaining a unified church in his commonwealth *at all*. All his passionate resentment at the power and influence of churches came to the fore in a remarkable series of chapters, and especially in Part Four of the book, subtitled 'Of the Kingdome of Darkness', in which the evil machinations of the clergy throughout the ages, and the pernicious consequences of their alliance with false philosophers (such as the Aristotelians), were exposed with savage irony. He put forward a vision of ecclesiastical history which was actually very close to a story Sarpi had told in some of his published works: free congregations of believers had been deceived into submitting their judgement to the pastors set over them, those pastors had then submitted to bishops, and finally the Pope had established an imperial sway over all ('the *Papacy*, is no other, than the *Ghost* of the deceased *Romane Empire*, sitting crowned upon the grave thereof' (ch. 47, p. 712)). But, at least in England, this structure had been dismantled in reverse order, beginning with the Reformation and culminating in the victory of the Independents. Hobbes celebrated their victory in a passage which, if one had not read it in *Leviathan*, one would attribute to Locke or one of the other great theorists of toleration:

> And so we are reduced to the Independency of the Primitive Christians to folow Paul, or Cephas, or Apollos, every man as he liketh best: Which, if it be without contention, and without measuring the Doctrine of Christ, by our affection to the Person of his Minister, (the fault which the Apostle reprehended in the Corinthians,) is perhaps the best: First, because there ought to be no Power over the Consciences of men, but of the Word it selfe, working Faith in every one, not alwayes according to the purpose of them that Plant and Water, but of God himself, that giveth the Increase: and

> secondly, because it is unreasonable in them, who teach there is such danger in every little Errour, to require of a man endued with Reason of his own, to follow the Reason of any other men, or of the most voices of many other men; Which is little better, than to venture his Salvation at crosse and pile . . . (ch. 47, p. 711)

The point is that, as I observed at the end of the previous section, in Hobbes's eyes the sovereign would not have the same kind of reasons for enforcing particular dogmas upon his citizens as churches historically had acted on in controlling their members. His right to enforce doctrine was essentially negative, and was intended above all to stop *non-sovereigns* from claiming such a right. As an example of what happened if churches (in this instance, the Church of Rome) got power over people, Hobbes referred to the most disturbing modern incident, the trial of Galileo:

> Our own Navigations make manifest, and all men learned in humane Sciences, now acknowledge there are Antipodes: And every day it appeareth more and more, that Years, and Days are determined by Motions of the Earth. Neverthelesse, men that have in their Writings but supposed such Doctrine, as an occasion to lay open the reasons for, and against it, have been punished for it by Authority Ecclesiasticall. But what reason is there for it? (ch. 46, p. 703)

This freedom of philosophical enquiry would be safer under a regime of separate churches, ruled by a doctrinally omnipotent civil sovereign, than under the traditional balance between Church and State.

But the theological implications of Hobbes's theory were even more radical than its implications for ecclesiastical organization. As we have seen, religious belief was for him a matter purely of faith. As long as this faith was a matter of believing in the independent validity of the historical record of Christianity, it could be seen as a reasonably conventional religious commitment. But as soon as faith became exclusively a matter of believing what the civil sovereign said, then, on most understandings of religion, Hobbes had ceased to have one at all. It was precisely this which the men who accused Hobbes of atheism picked on; as one of them said in 1669, 'if once it be taken for granted that the Scriptures have no Authority but what the Civil Power gave them, they will soon come, upon a divine account, to have none at all.' We can best express the change which had come over Hobbes by saying that for him all religion, including Christianity, had now become civil religion; whereas in his earlier works the Christian Church had offered an alternative to civil religion, the arguments of *Leviathan* destroyed that alternative.

Contemporaries were particularly sensitive to this because, as we have seen, they already had before their eyes the example of someone who argued that a society's religion should be purely a matter of civil politics, namely Machiavelli. He had horrified an earlier generation by claiming that Christianity was not a particularly satisfactory religion from a political point of view, and implying that something more like the religions of the ancient world would be better. Hobbes now seemed to be giving a philosophical justification for this cava-lier treatment of religious dogma. There were also plenty of people around in the 1650s and 1660s who were happy to read Hobbes in this way; a good example is Henry Stubbe, Hobbes's loyal follower at Oxford, who seriously considered the question of whether Islam might not on political grounds be a better religion for Western countries to adopt than Christianity.

Like Machiavelli or Stubbe, and unlike (say) Sarpi, Hobbes did not, however, argue that it might be desirable for a civil society to have *no* religion. In the Appendix to the Latin *Leviathan* (which was, admittedly, designed to meet his critics' objections), he argued that some religion was necessary for civil life, because of the utility of oath-taking (that is, promising to one's God) in order to maintain contracts and political allegiances (app. II, p. 352). But oath-taking, though important, was expressly presented in the body of the work as adding nothing to the force of contracts, so this argument must be treated with some reserve. What Hobbes consistently claimed was that a rational sovereign would organize *some* religion for his citizens as a means of worshipping the 'natural' God; but since that natural God was an impersonal creator about whom nothing could be truly predicated, this was as close to atheism as most contemporary readers could imagine. Hobbes's religious views were in the end most similar to those of Rousseau, the Jacobins, or the early nineteenth-century socialists.

But there was of course a certain irony in Hobbes's position. His general theory committed him not to any particular religious belief, but to the belief enforced by his sovereign (or to a free choice between the beliefs which his sovereign allowed to compete for support). But in seventeenth-century England, Hobbes alleged, the civil religion enforced by his sovereign was a Christianity based solely on the Scriptures. To demonstrate the coherence of his own intellectual position, therefore, Hobbes had fully to document the consistency of his general theory with Scripture. He had done this before, relatively superficially; but in *Leviathan* he tried seriously for the first time to wrestle with the problems posed to his metaphysics by the Christian belief that an eternal life awaited the true believer, and eternal damnation the ungodly.

His argument, as set out in Chapter 38 of *Leviathan*, is essentially that Christianity does not imply that there can be incorporeal existence. If Adam had not sinned, men would have lived on earth for ever; his sin (in some way Hobbes did not choose to analyse) caused mortality to fall upon the human race, but Christ's death redeemed mankind (again, Hobbes does not specify any of the mechanisms involved). Christ will return to earth at some time, to raise the dead and grant them back their material existence; he will then allow the godly to live for ever, but the ungodly he will condemn to a second, and this time final, death. There can be no independent life for men's 'souls': eternal life must require a body and a place of habitation. Such a view was not in fact completely outside the pale of Christianity: some early Christians believed something very similar, and in Hobbes's own time the heresy known as 'mortalism', which also asserted the impossibility of souls 'living' outside a body, had a number of adherents among radical Protestants (including, probably, John Milton).

But Hobbes's old friends greeted the theology of *Leviathan* with derision, and it is hard not to feel sympathy with them. A materialist apocalyptic vision of the kind set out in Chapter 38 is just about compatible with Christianity; but so much is left unexplained about what kind of physical process could possibly produce this result that it cannot be regarded as well integrated into Hobbes's general philosophy. As we have seen, Hobbes believed himself to be under a political obligation to produce a materialist Christianity, but the strain of the enterprise illustrates vividly the central dilemma of his (and, perhaps, *any* relativist or sceptical) approach.

This dilemma can be put in the following way. Hobbes's particular post-sceptical theory, like the sceptical theories of Montaigne and his followers, issued in the conclusion that one must obediently follow the laws and customs of one's country; Hobbes went further than Montaigne, in a way, since he argued in effect that one should *internalize* the laws and customs, and *really* believe them, or at least accept them as *intellectually* authoritative. But the laws and customs might include doctrines which were fundamentally incompatible with the principles upon which one was a relativist in the first place: what, then, should one do? Hobbes never resolved this dilemma, and it found expression in the deeply paradoxical fact that the great theorist of absolute submission to the power of the State lived the last years of his life in fear of being branded a heretic and atheist by that same State, while men who had taken up arms against it lived untroubled lives.

III Interpretations of Hobbes

Hobbes as a modern natural law theorist

Obviously, any philosopher of the stature of Hobbes plays a part in the construction of all subsequent philosophies. No successor can thoroughly ignore him, and even where they appear to do so (as, it has been argued, John Locke did) their silence is deeply expressive. Nevertheless, Hobbes's importance for later philosophers has fluctuated, and his works have not been read with the same care and attention throughout the 300 years between his death and our own time. In this part of the book, I shall survey the more important interpretations of Hobbes since his death, but I shall not attempt to give a complete history of his influence in modern philosophy, for such a history would amount in the end to a history of modern philosophy itself.

The first generation of serious and sympathetic readers of Hobbes were clear about his historical position. In the later seventeenth and early eighteenth centuries there were many attempts to write histories of modern philosophy, the first such works since antiquity. Their appearance signalled the fact that many contemporaries were conscious that something special and new had happened in the intellectual world, which could not be captured by using the categories left over from antiquity—categories such as 'Aristotelianism'. The first sketch of a history of modern moral philosophy was actually produced in Hobbes's lifetime by the German Samuel Pufendorf, who in 1672, in his *Law of Nature and Nations*, defended his own contentious ethical ideas by outlining what he took to be their origins. His sketch was then elaborated, largely by German and French writers, during the next fifty years, until it took the form of an absolutely standard account embodied in various textbooks and taken for granted by virtually everyone throughout Europe.

According to this history, modern moral philosophy began

with Hugo Grotius; he was 'the first to break the ice', in the words of one of these writers, after the long winter of Aristotelianism. Not only Aristotle, but all the theorists of antiquity and the Middle Ages, were flawed in central respects: as Pufendorf said, Aristotle's *Ethics*, 'which deals with the principles of human action, apparently contains scarcely anything other than the duties of a citizen in some Greek *polis*', and a similar charge of localism could be brought in some degree against other philosophers such as Cicero. The sceptics of antiquity, such as Carneades, and of modernity, such as Montaigne, all made this flaw abundantly clear, and it was Grotius's great merit that he was the first moral philosopher who fully engaged with the sceptical challenge and sought to answer it in a non-dogmatic way.

Grotius was followed in his enterprise, these histories continued, initially by two Englishmen. The first was John Selden, who published a vast and complex work on theories of natural law among the Jews; the second was Hobbes. The view of Hobbes put forward in these histories was, on the whole, a balanced and careful one. Pufendorf, for example, was critical of Hobbes's theology and of some of his ethics; but, he observed, many of the fundamental principles of modern moral philosophy 'would never have occurred to anyone had they not been in Hobbes's works' (Pufendorf was himself branded a Hobbist by some of his opponents for such remarks). The interpretation of Hobbes in the histories inspired by Pufendorf concentrated on what seemed to their authors to be the obvious facts that Hobbes took 'Self-Preservation, and Self-Interest, to be the original Causes of Civil Society' and that 'the Will of the Sovereign alone constitutes, not only what we call Just and Unjust, but even Religion; and that no divine Revelation can bind the Conscience, till the Authority, or rather Caprice, of his *Leviathan* ... has given it the Force of a Law' (These quotations are from an early eighteenth-century history by the Swiss Protestant Jean Barbeyrac). Consequently, there was general agreement that Hobbes was close to being an atheist, and was certainly at least a deist rather than a true Christian.

Despite all this, Hobbes was placed firmly in the middle of

the sequence of writers beginning with Grotius, and continuing through Pufendorf himself to culminate (revealingly) in John Locke. All these men were seen as in some sense working on a common enterprise. As will be apparent, this early account of seventeenth-century moral philosophy is close to the account put forward earlier in this book. It *is* in many ways reasonable to view Hobbes as someone who was trying to provide a persuasive theoretical foundation to the ethical ideas put forward by Grotius, and in the process transforming those ideas (at least to some extent); it *is* plausible to see Pufendorf and Locke as engaged on a similar task. Moreover, the late seventeenth- and early eighteenth-century view of Hobbes's religion has much to commend it. Though, as we have just seen, there was caution and ambiguity on the subject, no one regarded him as a conventional theist; in fact his underground reputation as an atheist led to the circulation in eighteenth-century France of avowedly atheistical tracts under his name. But such a reputation did not shift him from the pantheon of modern philosophers: considerable religious heterodoxy was virtually the norm among all the writers saluted in the eighteenth-century histories of modern moral philosophy.

On the other hand, there was no question in the minds of these historians that Hobbes argued for anything other than unlimited sovereign power. Though opponents of such untramelled authority might sympathize with the other figures in this 'modern natural law' tradition—notably, of course, Locke, but also Grotius and Pufendorf to some extent—they could never sympathize on this issue with Hobbes. We can see this in the different responses to Hobbes of eighteenth-century Englishmen. The Whig party which dominated eighteenth-century English politics saw itself as heir to the seventeenth-century radical tradition of opposition to absolute monarchy, and few Whigs enthused about Hobbes; their Tory opponents, on the other hand, were wedded to Anglican orthodoxy and were equally hostile to him. The one group who read Hobbes with open enthusiasm were the men who sought in some way to be 'above party', particularly the associates of the young King George III; and it was one of these, John Campbell (later to make his name as the chief propagandist for George's favourite, the Earl of Bute), who first collected Hobbes's English language moral and political works together in a handsome new folio edition (1750), with an introduction defending their author from calumny.

But such men were a relatively weak force; much more representative of the attitude to Hobbes, even among people who more than shared his religious heterodoxy, were the remarks of David Hume in his *History of England* (Hume was a supporter of the 'Rockingham Whigs', the administration which ousted Bute):

> In our time he is much neglected ... Hobbes's politics are fitted only to promote tyranny, and his ethics to encourage licentiousness. Though an enemy to religion, he partakes nothing of the spirit of scepticism; but is as positive and dogmatical as if human reason, and his reason in particular, could attain a thorough conviction in these subjects.

There was more, however, to this criticism of Hobbes than mere Whig prejudice. In the late eighteenth century the whole pantheon of modern philosophy was demolished, and on its ruins was erected quite another structure; and Hume was the man who began the process of demolition. His contemporary and (briefly) friend, Jean-Jacques Rousseau, continued it, and the final ground-clearing was accomplished by Immanuel Kant. Hume, in his *Treatise of Human Nature* (1739–40), was critical of all his natural law predecessors on the grounds that they had mistakenly tried to answer the sceptic by pointing to the actual universality of certain beliefs and practices—notably, the propensity to defend oneself and the belief that self-defence is morally legitimate. As Hume emphasized, no *evidence* of that kind could be relevant to the formation of anyone's own moral attitudes: it cannot follow from the fact that everyone else thinks or acts in a particular way, that *I* should do likewise. So the whole enterprise of modern natural law theory, with its emphasis on the facts of human psychology and culture, was itself vulnerable to a new kind of sceptical critique which denied the relevance of facts to ethical thinking. Not only

Hobbes, but also Grotius, Pufendorf, and Locke, shared in this new vulnerability. A similar point was made, though less explicitly, by Rousseau in his *Social Contract* (1762); as he said, men in a 'state of nature' could not be thought of as possessing moral rights or being under moral duties: morality was an invention of men in political communities, and could be authoritative only if those communities were properly founded democratic republics. Naturalistic ethics was thus a contradiction in terms.

Kant drew on both Hume and Rousseau to complete the criticism of eighteenth-century naturalism in all fields; but, far more than them, he explicitly repudiated the history of modern philosophy. In his eyes, Grotius and Pufendorf were 'sorry comforters' without any special intellectual role; the history of philosophy from antiquity down to his own time formed a single story, of a contest between what were later termed 'empiricists' and 'rationalists'—the former basing their arguments on sense-experience, the latter on mental concepts formed independently of experience. Kant's own philosophy was intended to locate this debate within a new context, and in particular to insist on the rigidity of the distinction between moral judgements and matters of fact. According to Kant, all the seventeenth-century writers thoroughly confused this distinction, mixing anthropology or psychology with ethics in an unjustifed way. Our moral judgements must come to us pure and uncontaminated by our beliefs about the material character of the world, including the character of human psychology.

The consequence of the rise of Kantianism (for Kant quickly became the model for the whole of Continental philosophy) was that the old history of moral philosophy was soon forgotten, the importance of Grotius and Pufendorf was overlooked, and the resemblance between Hobbes and the other natural law writers was disregarded. In post-Kantian histories (including, most strikingly, the *Lectures on the History of Philosophy* by Hegel), Hobbes is treated as a relatively minor contributor to an English 'empiricist' school of philosophers of which the most illustrious member was Locke. It should also be said that the seriousness with which Kant and his successors took the

Christian religion (in contrast to the insouciance of early eighteenth-century intellectuals) helped make them less impressed by Hobbes than the men of Pufendorf's and Barbeyrac's generation had been.

In England Kant's influence was far less; but here too the old heroes of modern philosophy were subjected to severe criticism, this time by the Utilitarians led by Jeremy Bentham, whose strictures on Grotius and Pufendorf in fact resemble those of Kant. Bentham chose Hume and Rousseau as his philosophical heroes, barely mentioning Hobbes; but later Utilitarians, and particularly Bentham's follower James Mill, came to see some of Hobbes's philosophy as anticipating their own. What the Utilitarians argued was that the different amounts of 'pleasure' or 'utility' which people get out of particular situations can be compared, and that public policy should be directed towards securing (in the famous phrase) 'the greatest happiness of the greatest number'. A necessary implication of this is that some people's interests or happiness might be sacrificed in the interests of wider utility, and that they might therefore have to be compelled politically to subordinate their concerns to those of the rest of the community.

It was this sense of the need for an omnipotent and neutral sovereign to bend citizens' wills to a Utilitarian norm which led the Utilitarian writers to read Hobbes with appreciation: Hobbes's own *moral* theory was very different from theirs, for there is no suggestion in Hobbes that one can meaningfully compare the utilities of different people, let alone subordinate one person's utility to a wider collective benefit. Hobbes was, as we have seen, a kind of liberal—that is, he believed that public policy should secure a particular level of welfare for all citizens (in his case, the level of bare survival), and that once that level is secured there should be no attempt to force policies upon the citizenry—though, as we have seen, extensive intervention in people's lives might in fact be necessary to secure the goal of universal survival. Moreoever, no one should be morally obliged to sink below that level (that is, to die) simply to allow more people the chance of living; yet the possibility of such a moral obligation is the essence of Utilitarianism. The

Utilitarian admirers of Hobbes thus borrowed his account of the right of the State to secure a social goal, but inserted their own account of what the social goal should be.

It was this Utilitarian interest that generated the first serious modern studies of Hobbes. What is still the standard edition of Hobbes's works (though a new edition is now gradually being put together at Oxford) was produced between 1839 and 1845 by William Molesworth, an MP and follower of the leading Utilitarian politicians of his day, George Grote and James and John Stuart Mill. The real relevance of Hobbes's ideas is shown strikingly by the fact that after Molesworth had supported the grant by the British government of an endowment for the Irish Roman Catholic college at Maynooth—a famous issue in the struggle against the remains of Anglican dominance of British public life—he was greeted by his Tory opponents when he stood for election at Southwark in 1845 with the cry of 'No Hobbes'! Grote and J. S. Mill were also mentors of the man who wrote the first scholarly modern biography of Hobbes, George Croom Robertson; his *Hobbes* (1886) is still well worth reading.

However, though (as Molesworth's experience at Southwark illustrates) the British State still encountered some opposition in its task of destroying the vestiges of *ancien régime* politics with which it was faced, its difficulties were as nothing compared to the problems faced by modern states on the Continent. It was an awareness of the relevance of Hobbes to these problems which led to a great revival of interest in him in Germany, in particular, and to the development of what is to this day the most authoritative and detailed study of Hobbes's intellectual development, that contained in the work of Ferdinand Toennies. In the years immediately after Bismarck's unification of Germany in 1870, many German socialists welcomed the new State as something which could in principle be used to advance the cause of socialism; whereas earlier socialists (such as Robert Owen in England) had been more like anarchists, highly wary of any incursions by the State into their socialist utopias, these German socialists thought that they could use the State to smash the forces of capitalistic exploitation, just as Bismarck had used it to smash artistocratic and ecclesiastical privileges.

Toennies was a follower of Ferdinand Lasalle, who argued along these lines, and he perceived that Hobbes could be used to provide a theoretical defence of using the State in this way: capitalistic enterprises and their competitiveness endangered social peace and individual liberty as surely as old religious feuding had done. From 1877 onwards he worked on Hobbes, making many manuscript discoveries in England (including notably the original manuscripts of the *Elements of Law*), and publishing the results of his labours in a series of articles and in a book of 1896. Gradually, like many other Germans, he came to lose confidence in the potential role of the State in promoting socialism, and he turned instead to a critique of the modern State in which Hobbes was the villain rather than the hero—he had ushered in a world of rationalistic, contractual relationships and had seen out a world of spontaneous communities. Socialism would now have to look back to the communities, and eschew the State. The sense that Hobbes was the genius of modernity, who invented the attitudes of what is called in German the *Gesellschaft*, the world of contract, and repudiated those of the *Gemeinschaft*, the world of community, has remained pervasive since Toennies— though Toennies also recognized that Grotius might equally qualify for this role. His approach to Hobbes was thus much closer in spirit to that of Hobbes's early readers than had been the case for more than a century.

Though Toennies himself concentrated on Hobbes's moral and political thought, his work on the Hobbesian manuscripts exposed the considerable range and power of Hobbes's philosophy of science. The first person to follow this up and carefully analyse the relationship between Hobbes and the other great early modern philosophers of science was a Dane, Frithiof Brandt, who published his work on *Thomas Hobbes's Mechanical Conception of Nature* in 1928 (Toennies read it in draft form and approved of it). Just as Toennies's studies have remained the basis of modern scholarship on Hobbes's political ideas, so Brandt's book has been the foundation for all subsequent work on Hobbes's philosophy of science. It was not until our own time that scholarship of this kind—the close investigation of Hobbes's relationships with his contemporaries and of the historical circumstances in which he composed his works—was applied once again to Hobbes. In this respect his fate resembles that of other great political theorists, for the period from about 1930 to about 1965 was remarkable for the widespread lack of interest in the kind of detailed and scholarly historical enquiry which had occupied the previous generation.

Hobbes as the demon of modernity

This is not to say, however, that the writers of the period 1930–65 had no interest in historical issues: the project of understanding Hobbes, and his relationship with broadly defined traditions of thought, continued, and produced most of the current interpretative literature on Hobbes. Indeed, Hobbes's allegedly special role in the creation of modernity, and what that might tell us about modern thought in general, has been at the heart of all these more recent discussions— though by no means all twentieth-century commentators on Hobbes have agreed that Hobbes was a characteristic representative of 'modern' thought.

The most striking examples of people who did think this are provided by two very different figures. One is the German (and, later, American) Leo Strauss, whose ideas on Hobbes were first put forward in a volume on *The Political Philosophy of Hobbes* (1934) and then in a series of lectures published under the title *Natural Right and History* (1953). The other is the Canadian C. B. Macpherson, who published an article on 'Hobbes's Bourgeois Man' (originally entitled 'Hobbes Today') in 1945, a book called *The Political Theory of Possessive Individualism* in 1962, and what is now the standard edition of *Leviathan* in 1968. I will deal with Strauss first.

Strauss had a vision of European intellectual history of some complexity and subtlety; put simply, he believed that there had always been a fundamental conflict between moral relativism, of the kind embodied in the ancient sceptical texts and in

Renaissance writers such as Montaigne, and the belief in 'natural right'. This latter belief was expounded most cogently by the post-Socratic ancient philosophers, who held, according to Strauss, that relativism could be combated through a process of philosophical reflection which sought to go beyond the superficial variety of belief and custom to an underlying unity of some kind. Strauss himself only hinted at what that unity might consist in, for it was part of his argument that only 'the wise' could see it; indeed it was this aspect of his theory, with its disconcerting implications about the role of 'the wise' in a community, which attracted both most support and most criticism from his readers.

The natural science of antiquity, Strauss argued, had assisted the anti-relativists by giving an account of human beings' natural ends which validated their moral duties. But the justifiable and inevitable collapse of that science in the seventeenth century had left the highest form of philosophy, scientific enquiry, detached from ethics, and allowed relativism a free rein once again. Hobbes's philosophy was thus the first modern moral philosophy, for it was the first fully to accept the implications of modern natural science. It restated ancient relativism in the form of a rights theory according to which men's natural rights express what they *want* to do, and natural law becomes derivative from the rights and barely a matter of duty at all.

However, Hobbes, according to Strauss, retained one 'single, but momentous idea' from the anti-relativists, namely the idea that a political philosophy is necessary and that there can be a 'best regime': he was not content merely to say that everyone as a matter of fact seeks to get what they want; he also wished to show that conduct of that kind is compatible with a 'good' social order. He made them compatible through his Leviathan State, just as Adam Smith later made them compatible through the hidden hand of the market; but this State rested on the 'fundamental fiction' that the will of the sovereign is the will of all, so it cannot really provide the answer to relativism.

Setting aside the highly contentious historical and moral background against which Strauss read Hobbes, there is undoubtedly some cogency to his interpretation. In particular, Strauss in my view correctly recognized that Hobbes subordinated natural laws to natural rights, taking the laws of nature to be general principles for the wise exercise of our rights. He also had a correct instinct for the central importance in this story of the relativistic or sceptical challenge, and for the ambiguity in Hobbes's relationship to that challenge—on the one hand seeking an answer to it, and on the other wishing to incorporate its basic insights into his own theory. The weakness in Strauss's argument lies in his often highly fanciful readings of the ancient writers rather than in his better grounded reading of Hobbes; but it has proved hard for modern scholars to disentangle that reading from its distasteful surroundings.

Strauss represents in a fairly extreme form the claim that Hobbes is the demon-king of modernity, but others have argued similar cases. The most interesting of these is, as I have said, C. B. Macpherson, who tried to argue that the distinctive character of Hobbes's political thought is due to his role as in some sense the spokesman for 'bourgeois' values. The congruence between some of Hobbes's philosophy and some of the attitudes of competitive mercantile capitalism has often been remarked on: in a way it was implied in Toennies's handling of Hobbes's historical role, and Strauss too observed (in opposition to Max Weber's well-known argument about the connection between Calvinism and the rise of capitalism) that it was Hobbes rather than his Calvinist opponents who appeared first to give voice to capitalistic attitudes. Put very broadly, there is an obvious plausibility about this position (if, again, we subsume Hobbes into a wider European tradition alongside Grotius and Locke): thus, for example, these writers *were* interested in breaking up associations within the State which might dominate or terrorize their members, and capitalists *were* often also interested in seeing such associations broken up if they hampered their own economic activities. Hobbes's polemic against guilds was part of a general polemic against particular associations or professional bodies, but it echoed similar complaints made by many prospectively competitive manufacturers.

The snag about Macpherson's view (which became even

more obvious when he tried to apply a similar argument to Locke) is that he regarded 'modern' man as *essentially* bourgeois, whereas the more wide-ranging and flexible historical sense of someone like Toennies recognized that some anti-bourgeois attitudes may also be part of modernity. As we saw, Toennies at one point proffered a socialist reading of Hobbes, and similar socialist readings of Locke were given in the nineteenth century. This is not to say that such readings are correct; it is rather to illustrate that the reading of Hobbes or Locke as capitalists is as plausible (or implausible) as the reading of them as socialists. Both capitalism and its critics have been part of modernity from the beginning, and a general philosophy of Hobbes's kind could—and did—appeal to both. Keith Thomas, in an article of 1965 ('The Social Origins of Hobbes's Political Thought'), pointed this out forcefully, observing, for example, that Hobbes's requirement on the sovereign to ensure the survival of the poorest in society, if necessary by taking away the property of the wealthier, runs counter to the most obviously 'bourgeois' enthusiasm, for inviolable private property.

Hobbes as a social scientist

While both Strauss and Macpherson wished (in their different ways) to emphasize the special modernity of Hobbes, most other writers in the later twentieth century have been dubious about this claim. Roughly speaking, there are two other traditions of thinking about Hobbes; we can understand both if we go back to the change introduced by Kant into the European sense of what philosophy is and has been. Whereas Strauss and Macpherson were in a way pre-Kantian in their view of the history of philosophy, those who have smoothed away Hobbes's modernity have been much more post-Kantian. (This might have been expected, given the way in which Kant himself dismissed the special character of seventeenth-century thought.)

The first of these two traditions has argued that Hobbes's theory was a theory of *prudence* or purely psychological motivation without any clear moral implications, and that this theory was simply the application to human conduct of principles of scientific enquiry well established long before Hobbes. According to this view, Hobbes's philosophy stands in the same relationship to modern ethical ideas as (say) Freudian psychology does: it provides a 'scientific' account of how men do, and perhaps how they must, behave, which the moralist has to take into account when making what used to be called 'value judgements'. But it does not itself supplant those ethical ideas, nor, fundamentally, was it intended to do so; though Hobbes, these writers have argued, may have thought that no value judgements were as a matter of fact possible. The second tradition has argued that Hobbes was a moralist, and what is more a moralist of the Kantian kind: that is, he really believed in moral judgements independent of factual assumptions about man's psychology.

As will have been clear from this book so far, I myself regard both these traditions as fundamentally mistaken; but writers within them have made a number of interesting and important interpretative points about Hobbes which must be taken seriously. I shall deal with the former tradition first.

Effectively, this tradition began with a book by Richard Peters in 1956 entitled *Hobbes*, and was carried on notably by J. W. N. Watkins in his *Hobbes's System of Ideas* (1965). Three propositions tended to be put forward by these writers. First, that Hobbes's political theory was intimately connected with his general scientific philosophy. Second, that his scientific method was the same as Galileo's, which was in turn a well-established principle of scientific enquiry (particularly popular at the University of Padua), namely the so-called 'resolutive-compositive method'. And third, that this was a method of empirical enquiry designed to elicit a moral or political science in the modern sense—something which could be used to explain human social behaviour.

Few people (other than those in the second of the post-Kantian traditions) would now disagree with the first of these propositions. It is true that Strauss, in his early book on Hobbes, devoted some scholarly effort to breaking the link between Hobbes's scientific writings and his political theory;

but given the general argument which he put forward later in *Natural Right and History*, it is not clear that he needed to make this break. As we have just seen, an interpretation of the rise of modern science is a key feature of that book. On the other hand, the actual account of the link which Peters and his successors gave is radically flawed by their universal reliance on the 'Short Tract', which they took to have been written *c.* 1630 and therefore to antedate any of Hobbes's political writings: as we saw earlier, there is no reason to suppose that the 'Tract' is by Hobbes. Their reliance on the 'Tract' also skewed their account of Hobbes's philosophy of science, for that work is not concerned to answer the sceptics, and it presents a much cruder materialism than anything found in Hobbes's non-contentious works.

The second point (which J. W. N. Watkins particularly stressed) was derived ultimately from the work of a great late nineteenth-century German neo-Kantian, Ernst Cassirer. He argued (in a book of 1906) that sixteenth-century late scholastic philosophers at Padua developed a scientific method in which objects were to be 'resolved' down to their component parts, the behaviour of those parts studied in a simplified form, and then the pieces 'composed' to make the whole again (the idea is roughly that to find what makes, say, a watch work, you take it to pieces and then put it together again). Cassirer argued that this was Galileo's experimental method, and following him these Hobbes scholars have claimed that it was Hobbes's also, resting their argument on one or two passages in his works where he speaks of explaining phenomena by 'resolving' them down into their parts, or by 'composing' them from basic principles. The most notable such passage, perhaps, is in the preface to *De Cive*, where Hobbes compares investigating 'the authority of the state and the duties of citizens' to examining the workings of a watch by dismantling it.

The view that this was Hobbes's method can be criticized on two fronts. First, it is not clear to modern scholars that Galileo's own method owed as much to this basically scholastic tradition as Cassirer thought; second, it is clear that it was not the most important way in which Hobbes approached the task of explaining physical events. As we have seen repeatedly, Hobbes did not believe that it was possible to have more than conjectural or hypothetical knowledge of the physical causes of any phenomenon; though mentally dismantling an object or event might help to generate or test such a hypothesis, it cannot ultimately give a better kind of knowledge of what is going on than one would gain simply by thinking about what might cause such objects or events in the first place.

The most important claim put forward by this group of writers was, however, the last one, that Hobbes's enterprise was in some way 'value-free'. Speaking of Hobbes's 'prescriptions'—that is, the rules derived from the laws of nature—Watkins, for example, wrote that 'my thesis is that Hobbes did derive his prescriptions from factual premisses but without committing a logical fallacy: for his prescriptions are not *moral* prescriptions—they are like "doctor's orders" of a peculiarly compelling kind' (*Hobbes's System of Ideas*, 1973). And he used Kantian categories to analyse Hobbes's laws of nature in this way.

In 1969 David Gauthier added a particular twist to this line of argument by analysing Hobbes's theory partly in terms of what is known as 'games theory', in his book *The Logic of Leviathan* (1969). Since the Second World War, economists and mathematicians have been interested in the formal analysis of a variety of 'games'—situations where two or more players try to get the best result they can for themselves by responding tactically in various ways to what the other players do. Some situations of this kind (as had long been recognized in informal discussions) present a paradoxical aspect, and the example of this paradox which has become standard in the literature is known as the 'Prisoners' Dilemma'. The idea is that two suspects are arrested by the police and put in separate cells. Each is then told that if both confess, they go to prison for a short period; if neither confesses, they will have to be released. But if only one confesses and incriminates the other, then he will be rewarded and his companion will go to gaol for a long time. The problem about this is that *whatever* each one of them does, it is in the interests of the other to confess: for if one confesses, it is better for the other also to confess and go to prison for a short time than to keep silent and be sentenced to a long imprisonment; while if one keeps silent, it is better for the other to confess and reap the reward than to keep silent and merely be released. So if the prisoners act rationally, they will both confess—but then they are both worse off than if they had each kept silent.

Gauthier was the first person to suggest that Hobbes's state of nature could be represented as a kind of Prisoners' Dilemma. Voluntary co-operation is not possible for men in a state of nature because they will always be better off defecting from a contract and seizing a unilateral advantage than sticking to the agreement. Only if their co-operation can be *compelled* in some way will they be motivated to abide by their agreements. Recognizing this fact about themselves and their fellows, men in a state of nature establish a sovereign who will, Gauthier argued, act on their behalf and exercise their natural rights to enforce obedience to contracts. The agreement to erect a sovereign is different from other agreements, since if everyone else abides by the contract, it is not in my interest to defect, since I will now be punished for doing so: we are thus no longer faced with the Prisoners' Dilemma which was characteristic of the state of nature. (We could draw an analogy with the prisoners: if they believed in the power of their Mafia boss to punish them for treachery, they would keep quiet.) It does however, remain the case that if we can get away with it, it must be in our interests to defect or break the sovereign's law; Gauthier acknowledged that this is a difficulty, particularly since Hobbes remarked in *Leviathan*, as we have seen, that only a 'foole' would hold that it could be right to do so.

The problem about this line of argument is partly that Hobbes was not actually concerned with explaining human conduct. As we have seen, Hobbes recognized that men can behave in ways quite contrary to the laws of nature, and these laws cannot therefore be explanatory in any straightforward sense. But we cannot take the other 'value-free' route of regarding the laws as prescriptions which tell us how (in modern terms) to 'maximize our utilities'. They are prescriptions which tell us how to exercise our right of self-preservation, but not how to do anything else; and self-preservation is important not simply because we all want to survive, but because it is the one thing we can be said to have the indubitable *right* to do—though the reason for that being the case is a fact about human psychology. If Hobbes is thereby indictable for having confused 'facts' and 'values' in some way, so be it: as we have seen, that very distinction was introduced partly as a criticism of writers like Hobbes. But it is not as obvious or as easy a distinction to make as these post-Kantian commentators have thought, and to reconstruct Hobbes's philosophy in such a way as to make him apparently aware of it may be as insensitive philosophically as it undoubtedly is historically.

To see the point of these remarks, we need only consider the difference between the account of the state of nature which I gave in Part II, and the account which Gauthier gave. According to my account, the problems of the state of nature arise, for Hobbes, *in the sphere of rights*: the state of war is the consequence of everyone implementing their right of self-preservation. Correspondingly, once a sovereign is established to co-ordinate the exercise of these rights, no one has the right to defect unless they believe incontrovertibly that their preservation is endangered by sticking to the contract (as in the case of the prisoner on his way to the gallows). They might want to defect, and their utility might be greater if they did so (for example, a burglar might be better off breaking the law than keeping it); but this is not the problem with which Hobbes was primarily concerned, nor were these the terms in which people were yet ready to write political theory.

For Gauthier, the state of nature involves the calculation of utilities by each inhabitant, and a choice between the best course of action, the next-best, and so on. On his view, there remains a puzzle about why, if we could be reasonably sure of not being caught, we should not break the sovereign's laws. On my view, this is not a problem for Hobbes, since we would have no *right* to break the law unless it was necessary for our preservation that we did so. Though we might benefit by breaking it, it would be an act *without right*, since rights (for

Hobbes) are limited to acts performed in the interests of self-preservation and do not extend to those rights which may satisfy our other wants. His objective was not to deliver a science of human behaviour of a non-moral kind, and many of the puzzles which have surfaced in the course of the modern discussions of such 'sciences' (like the Prisoners' Dilemma) are irrelevant to his inquiry.

Hobbes as a moralist

The idea that Hobbes was a moralist and not a value-free scientist was, of course, integral to the other tradition of thinking about Hobbes in the twentieth century; but the particular view of what a moralist must be which was enshrined in this tradition was highly misleading. It began with A. E. Taylor, in an article of 1938, 'The Ethical Doctrine of Hobbes', explicitly arguing that Hobbes was a kind of Kantian, as the Hobbesian laws of nature represent moral requirements upon men which are not founded in any way on the facts of human psychology; but the most famous and controversial statement of it was by Howard Warrender in a book published in 1957 entitled *The Political Philosophy of Hobbes: His Theory of Obligation*. Warrender's argument required him first to deny the connections between Hobbes's general philosophy and his moral or political theory; having narrowed his focus in this way, he turned to consider the distinction which Hobbes made in a number of passages, notably in Chapter 14 of *Leviathan*, between a *right* ('the liberty to do, or to forbeare') and a *law* (which 'determineth, and bindeth to one of them'). On the basis of this undeniable fact about Hobbes's terminology, Warrender then argued that since self-preservation is consistently described as a *right*, it could not be the foundation of the natural *law* to 'seek peace', since if we are free to protect ourselves *or to forbear from protecting ourselves*, no *obligation* can arise on us to protect ourselves.

Warrender then looked for some other source of obligation in Hobbes, and found it in the stray remarks which Hobbes made about the laws of nature being the commands of God. He concluded that according to Hobbes, we are morally obliged to obey God's commands simply because he is God (not because he has material power over us), and his commands require us above all to seek peace. If fulfilling God's instructions threatens our own survival, we are entitled to plead our natural right of self-preservation against the commands; but that right is not the foundation of our obligation to seek peace.

This subtle argument occasioned an immense amount of criticism in the 1950s and 1960s, much of which made the obvious but compelling point that on Warrender's account, Hobbes should have been the toast of seventeenth-century theists rather than the object of their deep suspicion. Yet these critics found it surprisingly difficult to provide an alternative explanation of the Hobbesian distinction between rights and laws. However, as we saw in Part II, an alternative explanation can be given, namely that our right of self-preservation is properly speaking a right *rationally to use our judgement about what conduces to our preservation*, and this right is indeed something we can 'forbear' from exercising—indeed, we partly forbear from exercising it when we establish a sovereign, for we then agree *not* to use our own judgement in a wide variety of cases. This is compatible with it being the case that the laws of nature provide (so to speak) permanent and incontrovertible judgements about what will lead to our preservation, and that they therefore in effect structure the way in which we rationally choose to exercise our right. If we put at the heart of our own reading of Hobbes's work his consuming interest in the disparities between different human beings' judgements and perceptions of the world, then Warrender's difficulties tend to disappear.

A somewhat different account of Hobbes as a moralist, though one of comparable or even greater subtlety, was provided by Michael Oakeshott, first in an introduction to an edition of *Leviathan* in 1945, and subsequently in an essay on 'The Moral Life in the Writings of Thomas Hobbes' (1960). What Oakeshott argued was essentially that Hobbes *defined* what is morally obligatory as *the commands of the sovereign*. The reason why men create a sovereign is that they are in some sense 'necessitated' or 'obliged' to do so by the laws of nature, given their natural fear of death; but this is not a 'moral' obligation—that is, it does not in any way take away natural moral rights. These natural rights are moral in character from the beginning: 'the natural Right of each man to all things . . . [is] inherent in the will, which is limitless in its claims.' But men are not by nature under any moral *obligation*. However, once the sovereign has been constituted, his will becomes a moral law for his subjects. Even the laws of nature, Oakeshott repeatedly said, could only become moral laws if the sovereign ordered his subjects to act upon them. What the sovereign says his subjects must do is not necessarily the same as their naked (non-moral) self-interest would have led them to do; his commands are therefore the same kind of thing as conventional moral principles—they depend for their force upon people's conviction about what they *ought* to do.

Thus, according to Oakeshott, Hobbes did not confuse facts and values; he simply had a rather unexpected view of what constituted the sources of morality, namely (for rights) the will of each person and (for laws) the will of a civil sovereign. In a sense, Oakeshott took seriously the description by Hobbes of the Leviathan as 'that *Mortall God*', for like God's will in what is called the 'voluntarist' tradition of medieval (and later) theology, the Leviathan's will constitutes right and wrong, and no further criterion is required. In another sense, Oakeshott's interpretation would make Hobbes very like Rousseau—for Rousseau undoubtedly did argue that the 'general will' of the civil association is the touchstone of moral truth, and that prior to their formation of the city, men in a state of nature are under no moral duties and have no moral rights. In a review of Strauss, Oakeshott did indeed link Hobbes to Rousseau, while in the introduction to *Leviathan* he linked him to the 'sceptical, late scholastic tradition' of voluntaristic nominalism.

The problem with Oakeshott's interpretation was partly, as a number of early critics observed, that it is hard to find clear textual evidence for it, but mostly that Hobbes does *not* base rights, either of individuals or of the sovereign, on 'limitless' wills. As we saw in Part II, Hobbes is very clear that 'the right to all things' is simply the right to do anything which is

111

thought to be necessary for self-preservation; many things we might *will* to do (such as getting drunk) are straightforwardly prohibited by the laws of nature, even in the state of nature. Oakeshott said of the laws of nature that they may put an internal, psychological 'impediment' upon a person, but that the person's 'natural Right to act in any way he chooses has suffered no impediment; fear and reason may limit a man's power, but not his Right'. But Hobbes said (in one of his clarificatory footnotes to *De Cive*) that

> there are some natural laws whose exercise does not cease even in war. For I do not understand how drunkenness or cruelty (that is, revenge which does not look to some future good) can conduce to peace, or the preservation of anyone. Briefly, in the state of nature, what is Just and Unjust is not to be assessed by the actions, but by the opinions and consciences of the agents. What is done out of necessity, in the interests of peace and one's own preservation, is done rightly. (III.27)

It seems clear that for Hobbes, natural rights can be limited by natural laws; or, more properly, that we do not have a natural right to act in any way we choose. It was in fact Spinoza who extended the idea of natural rights to cover all possible desires and actions, and he did so knowing that he was transforming Hobbes's theory.

Hobbes today

The current scholarship on Hobbes includes representatives, in various guises, of all the modern traditions dealt with above. But it has also begun to be more open to the historical peculiarities of Hobbes, and to be aware of the dangers of reading Hobbes too much through Kantian lenses. The process of recovering the historical Hobbes began, perhaps, with some influential essays by Quentin Skinner in the late 1960s, in which he argued among other things that Hobbes's theory had the same political *point* as those of a number of other (non-Hobbesian) writers who sought to defend allegiance to the new republic set up in England after 1649. These writers, known as

'Engagement theorists' after the 'Engagement', the oath to support the new regime which was required of people in 1650, argued that a new ruler in possession of the apparatus of government must be accorded the same obedience as the old ruler, whatever the route by which he had come to power; and Hobbes in the 'Review and Conclusion' to *Leviathan* did indeed clearly align himself with these theorists.

What Skinner's observation suggested was that a more detailed consideration of the actual interaction between Hobbes and the other theorists of his time, and their common response to political events, might repay examination, and much recent scholarship has followed his lead. Indeed, there is now a wealth of detailed work on Hobbes's life and writings not known since the time of Toennies and Brandt; the best indication of this is that Oxford University Press has begun to issue a new and properly based edition of all Hobbes's works (inspired to do so, it should be said, by Howard Warrender). At the same time, a general modern scepticism about the force of Kant's view of the history and task of philosophy has begun to affect interpretations of Hobbes; Skinner's work may indeed have been an intimation of this, and a recent book by Tom Sorell (though superficially resolutely non-historical) treats Hobbes's enterprise as a quest for a *moral science* of a suitably pre-Kantian kind. As we move into a world where scepticism has more appeal than Kant's 'moral law', the writings of the greatest and most consistent post-sceptic are bound to be studied with ever greater attention.

Conclusion

Hobbes's reputation, even in his own time, was a paradoxical one. He was seen as a fierce controversialist and a brusque dogmatist, yet his chief anger was directed at dogmatism of every kind. He was hostile to the intellectual authority of the churches, as expressed for example in the universities, yet he wanted his own philosophical works to be the authoritative texts within the universities. He praised toleration, yet he advocated an absolute sovereign with total power over intellectual matters. In this book I have tried to explain something of this paradox, but I have done so by placing Hobbes within a wider paradox, one which may be inherent in scepticism or liberalism. What happens if, like the men of Hobbes's generation and the generation immediately preceding, we lose all confidence in the truth of most existing beliefs? How do we actually *live*? This was a question which was put even in antiquity to the sceptics of the Graeco-Roman world, and it has remained the central question for sceptics ever since. The answer given by the writers of both the ancient world and the late sixteenth century was, essentially, live according to the laws and customs of your country; these laws and customs have no universal validity, but that is no reason for denying their practical hold upon you. Their scepticism thus became part of a deeply conservative, indeed timorous attitude to the ideological storm in which they found themselves.

As I have stressed, Hobbes's philosophy dealt with just these issues, and ended with broadly the same conclusion. Instead of scepticism, he offered *science*; but when one looks closer, one finds that his science is of an extremely exiguous kind. By clearing away all that he thought was doubtful, he was left with a bare a priori materialism, according to which the universe must consist of material objects causally interacting with one another, but the real character of these objects and their interactions is unknowable. Similarly in ethics: by clearing away all the complicated ethical theories of his orthodox predecessors (whether Aristotelians or humanists), he was left with nothing but the bare principle that we are morally entitled to preserve ourselves. Hobbes was left with little more to stand on as a guide to living than the sceptics like Montaigne, for they too had always acknowledged the practical force of the principle of self-preservation.

So it should come as no surprise that his conclusions were also close to theirs: that the laws of one's country are constitutive of one's general morality, and that whatever is necessary for one's preservation must be morally acceptable. He was prepared to take this position to remarkable lengths; for example, in one of the most outspoken passages in his entire works, he claimed (as we have already seen) that 'upon the occasion of some strange and deformed birth, it shall not be decided by Aristotle, or the philosophers, whether the same be a man or no, but by the laws' (*Elements of Law* II.10.8). Even the definition of what a human being is was thus put entirely at the disposal of the sovereign: there can be no objective 'fact of the matter' about it. The question of what a human being is, is still an urgent one: witness the intense debate about abortion. But we still appoint philosophers to head commissions to decide these issues, and are unwilling to take the implications of radical scepticism in these areas seriously, for, on Hobbes's account, it assigns to the State a kind of arbitrary power over the most important matters in our lives.

Yet many people would now pay at least lip-service to the sceptical relativism of Montaigne's generation. Scepticism about both science and ethics is more persuasive now than for many generations. Claims about the special validity of modern Western natural science have been undermined by the work of historians and philosophers of science, who have come to stress the culturally determined and unsubstantiated character of many scientific assumptions; while the literally ancient sense of the sheer multiplicity of human moral opinions, and of their incompatibility, has come once again to possess us. What is still not recognized sufficiently, however, is that Hobbes was one of the chief philosophers of our culture who faced both

115

these issues with intelligence and consistency; the only comparable figure is Hume, but it is not clear that Hume's answer to the question of how the sceptic ought to live is in the end more compelling than Hobbes's. Hume's answer was effectively, 'Do not take scepticism too seriously'—'A true sceptic will be diffident of his philosophical doubts, as well as of his philosophical conviction; and will never refuse any innocent satisfaction, which offers itself, upon account of either of them.' For that reason he accused Hobbes, as we have seen, of being really a dogmatist in the guise of a sceptic. But Hobbes did take both scepticism and philosophy seriously, and there was a kind of courage in his doing so which far outweighed his famous personal timorousness.

So if we do not like Hobbes's conclusions, we must still ask ourselves how far we have faced the full implications of the beliefs which we may well share with Hobbes. It is common nowadays for people to say that moral relativism should lead to a kind of liberal pluralism: that (say) the waning of religious dogmatism paved the way for modern religious toleration. But Hobbes's work illustrates that there is no reason why this should be so. Moral relativism, thought through properly, might lead instead to the Leviathan; and the Leviathan, while it will destroy older intolerances, may replace them by newer ones. We might baulk at that prospect, but we cannot by an act of will reinstate ourselves into the condition of firm belief, though (as Job found) it may be the only thing which can counteract the Leviathan. The sceptics of antiquity lived under the rule of absolute emperors; those of the Renaissance under absolutist monarchs. The rigid and alienating state structures of the modern world may also be an appropriate landscape for sceptics, and it is Hobbes who shows us why.

Notes on sources

The editions of Hobbes's works cited in the text are as follows:

The Elements of Law, Natural and Politic, ed. Ferdinand Toennies, 2nd edn by M. M. Goldsmith (London, 1969).

De Cive. The Latin Version, ed. Howard Warrender (Oxford, 1983). In view of the fact that the seventeenth-century English translation published as *De Cive. The English Version* (Oxford, 1983), and also ed. Warrender, is neither by Hobbes nor particularly accurate, I have used my own translations of the Latin text.

Thomas White's De Mundo Examined, tr. H. W. Jones (Bradford, 1976). This is a translation of the Latin text contained in *Critique du De Mundo*, ed. Jean Jacquot and H. W. Jones (Paris, 1973).

Leviathan, ed. C. B. Macpherson (Harmondsworth, 1968).

Extended quotations in the text from other than these works are from the following sources.

p. 6   C. Cornelius Tacitus, *Opera quae exstant*, ed. Justus Lipsius (Antwerp, 1574), the dedicatory letter to the Emperor Maximilian (my translation).

p. 7   Justus Lipsius, *Six bookes of politickes or civil doctrine . . . done into English by William Iones* (London, 1594), p. 62.

p. 8   Justus Lipsius, *Epistolarum Selectarum III Centuriae* (Antwerp, 1601), p. 234 (my translation).

p. 8   Michel de Montaigne, *Essayes*, tr. John Florio (Modern Library, London, n.d., p. 524).

p. 9   Pierre Charron, *Of Wisdome* (London, n.d. (before 1612)), sig. a7v.

p. 10   Francis Bacon, *Essays* (Everyman's Library, London, 1906), p. 52.

p. 18   Hobbes to the Earl of Newcastle in Historical Manu-
         scripts Commission, *13th Report II. Manuscripts of His
         Grace the Duke of Portland preserved at Welbeck
         Abbey* (1893), p. 130.

p. 36   Aubrey to Locke in *The Correspondence of John Locke*,
         vol. i, ed. E. S. De Beer (Oxford, 1976), p. 376.

p. 38   White Kennet, *A Sermon Preach'd at the Funeral of the
         Right Noble William Duke of Devonshire* (London,
         1708), p. 107.

p. 41   Hobbes, *Critique du De Mundo*, ed. Jean Jacquot and H.
         W. Jones (J. Vrin, Paris, 1973), p. 449

p. 43   Descartes, *Philosophical Writings*, vol. ii, tr. John Cot-
         tingham, Robert Stoothoff, and Dugald Murdoch (Cam-
         bridge, 1984), pp. 122–3.

p. 47   'The Questions concerning Liberty, Necessity, and
         Chance' in Hobbes, *The English Works*, vol. v, ed.
         William Molesworth (London, 1841), p. 55.

p. 50   'Considerations upon the Reputation, Loyalty, Man-
         ners, and Religion of Thomas Hobbes', in Hobbes, *The
         English Works*, vol. iv, ed. William Molesworth
         (London, 1840), p. 437.

p. 62   Sir Robert Filmer, *Patriarcha and Other Political Works*,
         ed. Peter Laslett (Basil Blackwell, Oxford, 1949), p. 242.

p. 77   Descartes, *Philosophical Writings*, vol. ii, tr. John Cot-
         tingham, Robert Stoothoff, and Dugald Murdoch (Cam-
         bridge, 1984), p. 131.

p. 93   The description of Grotius is from Jean Barbeyrac's 'An
         Historical and Critical Account of the Science of Moral-
         ity', annexed to his edition of Samuel Pufendorf's *The
         Law of Nature and Nations*, tr. Basil Kennet (London,
         1749), p. 67. Pufendorf's remark about Aristotle is from
         his *Specimen controversiarum circa jus naturale ipsi
         nuper motarum* (Uppsala, 1678), p. 9 and his remark
         about Hobbes from ibid. p. 13 (my translations).

p. 93 Barbeyrac, 'An Historical and Critical Account,' pp. 67 and 68.

p. 95 Hume, *The History of England*, vol. vi (Liberty Classics, 1983), p. 153.

p. 106 J. W. N. Watkins, *Hobbes's System of Ideas* (2nd edn, Hutchinson & Co., London, 1973), p. 51.

p. 111 Hobbes, *Leviathan*, ed. by Michael Oakeshott (Basil Blackwell, Oxford, n.d.), p. lviii.

p. 112 Ibid. p. lix.

p. 112 Hume, *A Treatise of Human Nature*, ed. L. A. Selby-Bigge (2nd edn revised by P. H. Nidditch, Oxford, 1978), p. 273.

Further reading

Hobbes's own writings

Although Oxford University Press is now producing a modern edition of Hobbes's collected works, it is a long way from completion: only *De Cive* has so far appeared. The only collected editions are thus *The English Works of Thomas Hobbes*, ed. Sir William Molesworth (11 vols., London, 1839–45) and *Thomae Hobbes . . . opera philosophica quae Latina scripsit omnia*, also ed. Molesworth (5 vols., London, 1839–45). There are also a number of important editions of particular works; in addition to those mentioned in the note on p. 117 above, there are the *Tractatus Opticus*, ed. F. Alessio, in *Rivista critica di storia della filosofia* 18 (1963), pp. 147–288; *De Homine*, partially translated in *Man and Citizen*, ed. Bernard Gert (Humanities Press, 1972); *Physical Dialogue*, tr. Simon Schaffer in S. Shapin and S. Schaffer, *Leviathan and the Air-Pump* (Princeton, 1985), pp. 345–91; *Behemoth*, ed. Ferdinand Toennies, 2nd edn by M. M. Goldsmith (London, 1969); *A Dialogue between a Philosopher and a Student of the Common Laws of England*, ed. Joseph Cropsey (Chicago, 1971); Quentin Skinner, 'Hobbes on Sovereignty: an unknown discussion', *Political Studies* 13 (1965), pp. 213–18; and Samuel I. Mintz, 'Hobbes on the Law of Heresy: A New Manuscript', *Journal of the History of Ideas* 29 (1968), pp. 409–14.

His letters

Hobbes's letters, often a very revealing source, have not yet been collected, but some of the more important are to be found in the following places: Historical Manuscripts Commission, *13th Report II. Manuscripts of His Grace the Duke of Portland preserved at Welbeck Abbey* (1893), pp. 124–30; Ferdinand Toennies, 'Siebzehn Briefe des Thomas Hobbes an Samuel Sorbiere', *Archiv fur Geschicte der Philosophie* 3 (1889–90), pp. 58–71, 192–232, 'Hobbes-Analekten', *Archiv fur Geschicte der Philosophie* 17 (1903–4), pp. 291–317, 'Hobbes-Analekten II', *Archiv fur Geschicte der Philosophie* 19 (1905–6), pp. 153–75, and 'Contributions à l'Histoire de la Pensée de Hobbes', *Archives de philosophie* 12

(1936), pp. 73–98; G. R. De Beer, 'Some Letters of Thomas Hobbes', *Notes and Records of the Royal Society* 7 (1950), pp. 195–206; and Marin Mersenne, *Correspondance* Vol. X, ed. Cornelis de Waard (Paris, 1967), pp. 210–12, 420–33, 487–506, 568–77, 588–91. Important letters connected with Hobbes are to be found in 'Illustrations of the State of the Church During the Great Rebellion', *The Theologian and Ecclesiastic* 6 (1848), pp. 161–75 (these include Payne's letters, referred to in Part I above), and Vittorio Gabrieli, 'Bacone, le Riforma e Roma nella versione Hobbesiana d'un carteggio di Fulgenzio Micanzio', *English Miscellany* 8 (1957), pp. 195–250.

His life

The account of Hobbes's life and the chronology of his writings presented in Part I is based in part on my own research, some of which is reported in 'Hobbes and Descartes' in G. A. J. Rogers (ed.), *Hobbes's Fourth Centenary* (Oxford, 1988). The most entertaining life of Hobbes is John Aubrey's in *Brief Lives*, ed. Oliver Lawson Dick (Harmondsworth, 1962), but a fuller account is given by G. C. Robertson's *Hobbes* (London, 1886). A. Rogow, *Thomas Hobbes* (New York, 1986), is more up to date, but should be used with some caution. Useful material about particular episodes in Hobbes's life is to be found in J. Jacquot, 'Sir Charles Cavendish and his Learned Friends', *Annals of Science* 8 (1952); J. J. Hamilton, 'Hobbes's Study and the Hardwick Library', *Journal of the History of Philosophy* 16 (1978); N. Malcolm, 'Hobbes, Sandys and the Virginia Company', *Historical Journal* 24 (1981); Q. R. D. Skinner, 'Thomas Hobbes and his Disciples in France and England', *Comparative Studies in Society and History* 8 (1966), and 'Thomas Hobbes and the Nature of the Early Royal Society', *Historical Journal* 12 (1969). The interesting iconography of Hobbes's works is discussed in M. M. Goldsmith, 'Picturing Hobbes's Politics?', *Journal of the Warburg and Courtauld Institutes* 44 (1981) and Keith Brown, 'The Artist of the *Leviathan* Title-page', *British Library Journal* 4 (1978).

His intellectual context

The intellectual context in which I have located Hobbes is best studied through the writings of Descartes, *Philosophical Writings*,

Further reading

tr. John Cottingham, Robert Stoothoff, and Dugald Murdoch (Cambridge, 1984); Hugo Grotius, *De Iure Belli ac Pacis* tr. F. W. Kelsey (Oxford, 1925); and John Selden, *Table Talk*, ed. Frederick Pollock (London, 1927). I have discussed the context in my 'The "Modern" Theory of Natural Law' in *The Languages of Political Theory in Early-Modern Europe*, ed. Anthony Pagden, (Cambridge, 1987) and, in a somewhat different way, in my *Natural Rights Theories* (Cambridge, 1979).

His general philosophy

There are not many reliable accounts of Hobbes's general philosophy; the best are probably Richard Peters, *Hobbes* (Harmondsworth, 1956); Tom Sorell, *Hobbes* (London, 1986) and J. W. N. Watkins, *Hobbes's System of Ideas* (2nd edn, London, 1973). Two useful collections of essays on various aspects of Hobbes's thought are K. C. Brown (ed.), *Hobbes Studies* (Oxford, 1965); M. Cranston and R. Peters (eds.), *Hobbes and Rousseau: A Collection of Critical Essays* (New York, 1972).

Scientific ideas

On Hobbes's specifically scientific ideas, see above all F. Brandt, *Thomas Hobbes's Mechanical Conception of Nature* (Copenhagen, 1928) and A. Pacchi, *Convenzione e ipotesi nella formazione della filosofia naturale di Thomas Hobbes* (Florence, 1965). S. Shapin and S. Schaffer have discussed Hobbes's disputes with Boyle and Wallis in *Leviathan and the Air-Pump* (Princeton, 1985), and A. E. Shapiro has given a careful account of Hobbes's optics in 'Kinematic Optics: A Study of the Wave Theory of Light in the Seventeenth Century', *Archive for the History of the Exact Sciences* 11 (1973).

Ethics and politics

Modern writers on Hobbes's ethics and politics fall largely into the groups discussed in Part III above. Those who take Hobbes to be representative of modernity include C. B. Macpherson in his edition of *Leviathan*, his essay 'Hobbes's Bourgeois Man', repr. in Brown, *Hobbes Studies*, and his *The Political Theory of Possessive Individualism: Hobbes to Locke* (Oxford, 1962), and Leo Strauss: his chapter on Hobbes in *Natural Right and History* (Chicago,

1953) is also reprinted in *Hobbes Studies,* and he earlier devoted an entire book to Hobbes, *The Political Philosophy of Hobbes. Its Basis and Genesis* (Oxford, 1936).

Writers who look on Hobbes as a kind of social scientist include Peters, and Watkins; M. M. Goldsmith in his *Hobbes's Science of Politics* (New York, 1966); F. S. McNeilly in *The Anatomy of Leviathan* (London, 1968), and David Gauthier in *The Logic of Leviathan* (Oxford, 1969). An elegant recent work influenced by Gauthier is Jean Hampton, *Hobbes and the Social Contract Tradition* (Cambridge, 1986).

The principal writers who look on Hobbes as a moralist are A. E. Taylor, whose essay on Hobbes is reprinted in Brown's *Hobbes Studies;* F. C. Hood in *The Divine Politics of Thomas Hobbes* (Oxford, 1964); M. Oakeshott in *Hobbes on Civil Association* (Oxford, 1975), a collection of his earlier essays on Hobbes, including his famous introduction to *Leviathan;* and Howard Warrender in *The Political Philosophy of Hobbes. His Theory of Obligation* (Oxford, 1957). Warrender also published a useful summary of his views in Brown's *Hobbes Studies.* The controversy about Warrender is best studied in that collection, with the addition of Thomas Nagel, 'Hobbes's Concept of Obligation', *Philosophical Review* 68 (1959), and Q. R. D. Skinner, 'Hobbes's Leviathan', *Historical Journal* 7 (1964). A careful work on Hobbes's ethics which stands somewhat apart from these arguments is D. D. Raphael, *Hobbes. Morals and Politics* (London, 1977).

Useful studies of particular issues in Hobbes's political thought include R. Ashcraft, 'Hobbes's Natural Man', *Journal of Politics* 33 (1971); M. Missner, 'Skepticism and Hobbes's Political Philosophy', *Journal of the History of Ideas* 44 (1983); two related essays by Q. R. D. Skinner, 'The Ideological Context of Hobbes's Political Thought', *Historical Journal* 9 (1966), and 'Conquest and Consent: Thomas Hobbes and the Engagement Controversy' in *The Interregnum*, ed. G. E. Aylmer (London, 1972); and C. D. Tarlton, 'The Creation and Maintenance of Government: A Neglected Dimension of Hobbes's *Leviathan*', *Political Studies* 26 (1978). David Johnston has published an important study of Hobbes's attitude towards the political implications of rhetoric in *The Rhetoric of Leviathan. Thomas Hobbes and the Politics of Cultural Transformation* (Princeton, 1986).

Further reading

Religious ideas

So far, there is remarkably little of quality written on Hobbes's religious ideas. The four most useful essays are E. J. Eisenach, 'Hobbes on Church, State, and Religion', *History of Political Thought* 3 (1982); R. J. Haliday, T. Kenyon, and A. Reeve, 'Hobbes's Belief in God', *Political Studies* 31 (1983); J. G. A. Pocock, 'Time. History and Eschatology in the Thought of Thomas Hobbes' in *Politics, Language and Time* (London, 1972); and A. Ryan, 'Hobbes, Toleration, and the Inner Life' in *The Nature of Political Theory*, ed. D. Miller (Oxford, 1983).

His influence

Hobbes's influence on other writers, and his reputation among contemporaries, is traced by J. Bowles in *Hobbes and his Critics. A Study in Seventeenth-Century Constitutionalism* (London, 1951); F. M. Coleman, *Hobbes and America. Exploring the Constitutional Foundations* (Toronto, 1977); S. I. Mintz, *The Hunting of Leviathan. Seventeenth Century Reactions to the Materialism and Moral Philosophy of Hobbes* (Cambridge, 1962); and P. Russell, 'Hume's Treatise and Hobbes's *The Elements of Law*', *Journal of the History of Ideas* 46 (1985).

Index

125

Index

OXFORD

MORE OXFORD PAPERBACKS

Details of a selection of other Oxford Paperbacks follow. A complete list of Oxford Paperbacks, including The World's Classics, Twentieth-Century Classics, OPUS, Past Masters, Oxford Authors, Oxford Shakespeare, and Oxford Paperback Reference, is available in the UK from the General Publicity Department, Oxford University Press (RS), Walton Street, Oxford, OX2 6DP.

In the USA, complete lists are available from the Paperbacks Marketing Manager, Oxford University Press, 200 Madison Avenue, New York, NY 10016.

Oxford Paperbacks are available from all good bookshops. In case of difficulty, customers in the UK can order direct from Oxford University Press Bookshop, 116 High Street, Oxford, Freepost, OX1 4BR, enclosing full payment. Please add 10 per cent of the published price for postage and packing.

BURKE

C. B. Macpherson

This new appreciation of Edmund Burke introduces the whole range of his thought, and offers a novel solution to the main problems it poses. Interpretations of Burke's ideas, which were never systematized in a single work, have varied between apparently incompatible extremes. C. B. Macpherson finds the key to an underlying consistency in Burke's political economy, which, he argues, is a constant factor in Burke's political reasoning.

'Professor Macpherson . . . teases out the strands in Burke's thought so carefully that one comes to understand, not only Burke himself, but his interpreters.' *Times Educational Supplement*

Past Masters

CARLYLE

A. L. Le Quesne

A. L. Le Quesne examines the views of this first and most influential of the Victorian 'prophets', explaining how his greatness lay in his ability to voice the needs of a remarkably moral generation.

'A first-rate introduction . . . it is not the least of the merits of this excellent short study that it shows some of the tensions yet to be found in reading Carlyle.' *Edinburgh University Journal*

Past Masters

COBBETT

Raymond Williams

Raymond Williams begins his book with a portrait of this extraordinary man, in one lifetime a soldier, a journalist, a farmer, and a political activist. But behind Cobbett's considerable personality lay important ideals and ideas. Professor Williams discusses these, and in particular Cobbett's views on poverty and property, on liberty, and on education, emphasizing the development of his outlook and identifying important shifts. He places Cobbett in context in the history of radical thought, and establishes the lasting importance of his tireless contributions to the debate about how society should be organized.

Past Masters

ENGELS

Terrell Carver

In a sense, Engels invented Marxism. His chief intellectual legacy, the materialist interpretation of history, has had a revolutionary effect on the arts and social sciences, and his work as a whole did more than Marx's to make converts to the most influential political movement of modern times. In this book Terrell Carver traces Engel's career, and looks at the effect of the materialist interpretation of history on Marxist theory and practice.

'Carver's refreshingly honest book . . . is packed with careful judgements about the different contributions of Engels to 19th century marxism.' *New Society*

Past Masters

HEGEL

Peter Singer

Many people regard Hegel's work as obscure and extremely difficult, yet his importance and influence are universally acknowledged. Professor Singer eliminates any excuse for remaining ignorant of the outlines of Hegel's philosophy by providing a broad discussion of his ideas, and an account of his major works.

'An excellent introduction to Hegel's thought . . . Hegel is neatly placed in historical context; the formal waltz of dialectic and the dialectic of master and slave are economically illumined; Singer's use of analogy is at times inspired.' *Sunday Times*

Past Masters

MACHIAVELLI

Quentin Skinner

Niccolò Machiavelli taught that political leaders must be prepared to do evil that good may come, and his name has been a byword ever since for duplicity and immorality. Is his sinister reputation really deserved? In answering this question Quentin Skinner focuses on three major works, *The Prince*, the *Discourses*, and *The History of Florence*, and distils from them an introduction of exemplary clarity to Machiavelli's doctrines.

'without doubt the best short account of the author of *The Prince* that we are likely to see for some time: a model of clarity and good judgement' *Sunday Times*

'compulsive reading' *New Society*

Past Masters

MARX

Peter Singer

Peter Singer identifies the central vision that unifies Marx's thought, enabling us to grasp Marx's views as a whole. In plain English he views him as a philosopher primarily concerned with human freedom, rather than as an economist or social scientist. He explains alienation, historical materialism, the economic theory of *Capital,* and Marx's idea of communism, and concludes with a balanced assessment of Marx's achievement.

'an admirably balanced portrait of the man and his achievement'
Observer

Past Masters

MILL

William Thomas

Basing his study on a detailed assessment of the way in which Mill was influenced by his upbringing, William Thomas traces the main ethical, economic, and psychological doctrines which underpin Mill's work, and offers an unusual interpretation of the origins and development of his mature philosophy.

'there is much stimulating material here both for the beginning student and for the Mill scholar . . . as an introductory piece on Mill, the book has great merit. It contains a wealth of useful information about Mill's life and contemporaries, and Thomas is strong on the social and political history of the period, which is so often ignored yet which is so crucial to a full understanding of Mill's thought.' Susan Mendus, *Times Higher Educational Supplement*

Past Masters

MONTESQUIEU

Judith N. Shklar

Charles Louis de Secondat, Baron de Montesquieu (1689–1755) was perhaps the most authentic of the political thinkers of the Enlightenment. He believed passionately in toleration and in the moral benefits of science, and constructed a naturalistic system of political science based on a study of history, comparitive government, and psychology. His *magnum opus* is undoubtably *The Spirit of the Laws* (1748), which examines the concept of law as both cause and effect of the structure of political systems.

Inspiring everything he wrote was a profound hatred for, and fear of, despotism, which he regarded as the supreme evil, and which served him as a moral standard for judging regimes. Of those, he considered England the best modern example, and his account of its constitution which was to provide a model for the American constitution of 1787, inspired many of the French liberals of his day.

Past Masters

MORRIS

Peter Stansky

William Morris was one of the great figures of the Victorian age: an artist and craftsman and a successful writer of romances. He was also an ardent socialist and leader of the labour movement. His concern for the place of art in society and his analysis of that society's discontent place him as a thinker in the company of Marx and Ruskin. Peter Stansky presents, in the context of his age and in all his engaging multiplicity, the life and personality of a man whom a contemporary perceptively described as 'The Earthly Paradox'.

'warmly commended' E. P. Thompson, *History Today*

Past Masters